Praise for *Mapping Leadership*

Mapping Leadership provides a thoroughly readable, practical guide that makes sense of a large body of research on school leadership. It moves attention away from the leader as an individual to the developer of systems of collaboration. Using tangible examples, the book vividly demonstrates the process of school improvement.

—**Elaine Allensworth,**
Lewis-Sebring Director, University of Chicago Consortium on School Research

The depth and utility of this book are incredible. I love how the CALL surveys exemplify a range of possible practices. The detailed descriptions in each chapter allow administrators to map what they do against exemplary leadership behaviors. This book is a gift to the field of educational leadership. I can't recommend it highly enough.

—**Scott McLeod,**
Associate Professor, University of Colorado Denver, and Founding Director, CASTLE

Many practicing school leaders, especially principals, find themselves drowning in research on an endless list of education topics. Despite all that is available, leaders still struggle with knowing *how* to shape sustainable improvements and *what tasks* are essential for getting there. This book is an invitation to explore distributive leadership and to develop the practices necessary for growing capacity and improving learning for all. I can't imagine a better guide for any leader wanting to think and act differently. The book is your map for an improved future. Use it and share it now!

—**Patricia Neudecker,**
Director, Administrative Leadership Programs, School of Education, Alverno College,
Milwaukee, Wisconsin

Richard Halverson
Carolyn Kelley

MAPPING LEADERSHIP

The Tasks That Matter for Improving
Teaching and Learning in Schools

JB JOSSEY-BASS™
A Wiley Brand

Published by Jossey-Bass

A Wiley Brand

One Montgomery Street, Suite 1000, San Francisco, CA 94104–4594—www.josseybass.com

The research reported in this paper was supported by the U.S. Department of Education Institute of Education Sciences (Award R305A090265) and by the Wisconsin Center for Education Research, School of Education, University of Wisconsin-Madison. Any opinions, findings, or conclusions expressed are those of the authors and do not necessarily reflect the views of the funding agencies, WCER, or cooperating institutions.

Jossey-Bass books and products are available through most bookstores. To contact Jossey-Bass directly call our Customer Care Department within the U.S. at 800–956–7739, outside the U.S. at 317–572–3986, or fax 317–572–4002.

Wiley publishes in a variety of print and electronic formats and by print-on-demand. Some material included with standard print versions of this book may not be included in e-books or in print-on-demand. If this book refers to media such as a CD or DVD that is not included in the version you purchased, you may download this material at http://booksupport.wiley.com. For more information about Wiley products, visit www.wiley.com.

Library of Congress Cataloging-in-Publication Data

Names: Halverson, Richard, author. | Kelley, Carolyn, author.
Title: Mapping leadership : the tasks that matter for improving teaching and
    learning in schools / Richard Halverson, Carolyn Kelley.
Description: San Francisco, CA : Jossey-Bass ; Hoboken, NJ : John Wiley &
    Sons, 2017. | Includes bibliographical references and index.
Identifiers: LCCN 2017005480 (print) | LCCN 2017009353 (ebook) | ISBN
    9781118711699 (pbk.) | ISBN 9781118711514 (Adobe PDF) | ISBN 9781118711576 (ePub)
Subjects: LCSH: Educational leadership.
Classification: LCC LB2806 .L324 2017 (print) | LCC LB2806 (ebook) | DDC
    371.2—dc23
LC record available at https://lccn.loc.gov/2017005480

Cover design: Wiley

Cover image: © Mr Plumo/iStockphoto-Compass Icon, © Yuri_Arcurs/iStockphoto-Urban Underground

Printed in the United States of America

FIRST EDITION

PB Printing 10 9 8 7 6 5 4 3 2 1

To our daughters

CONTENTS

ABOUT THE AUTHORS

Richard Halverson is a Professor of Educational Leadership and Policy Analysis in the UW-Madison School of Education. His research aims to bring the research methods and practices of the Learning Sciences to the world of educational leadership and interactive media. Rich co-directs the Wisconsin Collaborative Education Research Network and the Comprehensive Assessment of Leadership for Learning project, and was a co-founder and co-director the Games + Learning + Society Research Center. He is a former high school teacher and administrator, and earned an MA in Philosophy and a PhD in the Learning Sciences from Northwestern University. He is co-author (with Allan Collins) of *Rethinking Education in the Age of Technology: The Digital Revolution and Schooling in America.*

Carolyn Kelley is Senior Associate Dean for Academic Programs in the School of Education at the University of Wisconsin-Madison, and the Jim and Georgia Thompson Distinguished Professor of Education in the Department of Educational Leadership and Policy Analysis. Her research focuses on educational policy and strategic human resources management in schools, including leadership development, principal and teacher evaluation, and teacher compensation. She co-directs the Comprehensive Assessment of Leadership for Learning project, and is co-author (with Jim Shaw) of *Learning First! A School Leader's Guide to Closing Achievement Gaps.*

ACKNOWLEDGMENTS

It has been a great journey to build and share CALL over the years. The Comprehensive Assessment of Leadership for Learning project was the result of partnerships with colleagues over the past dozen years. We are grateful to the staff at the U.S. Department of Education Institute of Education Sciences (award R305A090265) and our program officer, Katina Stapleton, for their support on this work.

Our original CALL research group helped to define the project as a new way to think about supporting school leadership practice. Eric Camburn played a central role in leading the CALL validation process. Matt Clifford helped to connect us with a national audience for CALL and provided invaluable ongoing technical and intellectual support. Jim Shaw, Tony Milanowski, and Steve Kimball provided crucial practical and technical insights to get the project off the ground, and Peter Goff and Alex Bowers gave us the expertise and organizational skills to unlock what CALL was telling us about leadership practices at scale.

The CALL project allowed us to meet and support the education of an extraordinary group of graduate researchers, including Jason Salisbury, Marsha Modeste, Seann Dikkers, and Shree Durga. We especially thank Mark Blitz, whose dedication, vision, and hard work guided CALL through the design process to result in a vibrant school reform tool with a nationwide following. Also, thanks to Mark for his excellent insights that sparked our thinking in Chapter 7.

CALL would not have been possible without the collaboration of our partner schools across Wisconsin and the rest of the United States. In particular, we thank the School Leadership Network; the Georgia Leadership Institute for School Improvement; WestED; the Oakland (California) School District; the Racine Unified, Lake Mills, Burlington, and Madison Metropolitan School districts in Wisconsin; the Wisconsin Cooperative Educational Service Agencies; and the School Administrators Institute for Transformational Leadership. Thanks to

Helle Bjerg and Søren Hornskov for their interest and support for translating CALL into Danish and sharing it with their colleagues across Denmark. We are grateful to Jim Lynch and Joe Schroeder from the Association of Wisconsin School Administrators and Kurt Kiefer and Sheila Briggs of the Wisconsin Department of Public Instruction. We thank Matt Messinger in the Wisconsin Center for Education Products and Services for his patience and support in guiding CALL through the transition from a research project to a viable market product. We also thank Louis Condon and Laura Dunek for their good humor and invaluable legal advice and support through this transition.

The team at Jossey-Bass has been supportive and patient throughout the process of developing this book. Thanks to the reviewers who helped us to refine and focus our message. Thanks to Julie Kallio and Sarah Hackett for their preparation of the CALL data and organizational help with the manuscript. Special thanks to Julie for her keen eye in poring over the final manuscript and references. We thank the University of Wisconsin-Madison School of Education, the Educational Leadership and Policy Analysis Department, the Wisconsin Center for Education Research, the University of Wisconsin Survey Center, and the Learning Games Network for their expertise and support. We also thank the Institute for Learning at the University of Pittsburgh, the Wallace Foundation, and the partner institutions in the Wallace project for their support in the development of our initial thinking about the tasks of distributed leadership in schools.

We thank Frank, Sarah, Nate, Erica, Gracie, Nick, and Katja for, well, everything. We especially thank Erica Halverson for reading and providing feedback on every painful page of the early drafts of the book. Thank you so much!

PROLOGUE

Wow, that was quite a year, thought Truman High School principal Trina Meadows. As she breathed a sigh of relief and stretched out at her desk, she listened to the quiet that meant the end of another school year. The last group of teachers, the science team, had just checked out for the end-of-the-year room inspection, and now the school year had officially come to a close.

It was a pretty successful year, all things considered. Graduation went well, with many hugs and mercifully few pranks. Only 35 of the 650 seniors did not make it through the year, a remarkable improvement over the 25% of seniors who did not make it to graduation when Meadows came to the school as principal three years earlier. Not only were the graduation rates going up, but ACT scores and college placement rates were starting to look promising. The gains were not evenly shared across the student community—the special education students continued to struggle to make progress—but there seemed to be a shared sense of progress being made in the school and the teachers were coming together as a staff, committed to improving learning for all students.

Also, it looked as if most of the staff would come back in the fall. Of course, the usual number of last-minute replacements would need to be made, but the new hiring and retention processes Meadows and the district leadership team had developed seemed to be making a difference. Meadows and her team had met with each of the parents whose children were involved in summer school beginning in two weeks, and she thought she could finally catch her breath.

As she relaxed into her chair, she was drawn to a copy of the school's strategic plan posted next to her window. She leaned forward and opened the top folder on the pile to the list of initiatives that had guided Truman's leadership agenda this past year. It was an impressive list, thought Meadows; she and her staff had accomplished good work. In addition to educating 2,200 students, her team had designed and implemented a new data system that would document teacher practices toward their professional learning goals, a new discipline program, a personalized learning initiative for students to develop study and time management skills, a transportation plan to involve all families in school activities, and a new hands-on science curriculum that got students and teachers out into the community. Many students, teachers, and community members cared deeply about these initiatives, and Meadows was proud of the ways her team channeled their desire to improve teaching, learning, and support into meaningful programs for students.

Meadows's thoughts turned to the new restorative justice program. Truman's teachers worked with the guidance staff to develop a program for students to make amends instead of submitting to the traditional disciplinary program. Truman guidance staff reported that the zero-tolerance discipline policies that Meadows and her staff had inherited had the unintended consequence of overpunishing the school's Spanish-speaking students. The department chairs and the guidance team suggested restorative justice as a path for students to learn about their obligations to the community and to make good on the harm their behavior had caused. At first, a few parents spoke in the press about their fears of declining behavioral standards in the school, but Meadows explained how the new program was beginning to work by inviting students to address the consequences of their actions. Meadows was proud of the efforts that students, staff, and teachers had made over the year to transform the school climate. *What is our next step?* wondered Meadows. *How can we build on the promising start of the restorative justice initiative?*

As she reviewed the other initiatives on the list, she reflected on the new teacher evaluation system. The district data team was excited about using this approach to help teachers track their learning goals. At first, Meadows was nervous about this approach: it sounded too much like surveillance, and many of the teachers shared her concerns. Still, a group of math teachers volunteered to use the system to collect data on their professional learning plans, and Meadows was surprised at how the math department meetings began to focus on classroom practice and discussions about what kinds of data should count as evidence for learning. Seeing these good practices in action led Meadows to wonder how to get some of the other departments to participate in the same way.

The other programs on the list led her to similar reflections: each of the new initiatives was built on good research and brought together faculty and staff around common problems that needed to be solved. Meadows thought that she had developed a strong professional community across the school around improvement. She led the effort to develop a shared vocabulary for talking about practice and reform, building on the district initiative to use the right kinds of information to guide their work. Since coming to Truman, she had made a commitment to be out in the school every day, visiting classrooms and making connections with teachers, staff, students, and families so that she was school community. She knew that her colleagues in several other district schools were envious of the community she had built at Truman, and the results her team was seeing made it easier to get support from the district and from families and businesses in the community. *It was a good year*, she thought, and she should celebrate a job well done.

Lingering over this pile of reports, though, began to make Meadows feel a little uneasy about the road ahead. Although she and her staff had made progress, many problems remained to be solved. Some of the new programs started at Truman seemed to be working, but in other areas, there were big gaps that Meadows had struggled to address. For example, the school had started a new study skills program two years ago when several teachers spoke up about how to support students who needed the most help. It was pretty clear, though, that many teachers did not know about the program and that many of the students who could benefit from it were not involved. Meadows also knew that addressing student learning at the level of study skills did not really get at the real issue: improving classroom teaching. She struggled with how to reconcile the group of educators who wanted a short-term solution with the others who felt that shortcuts would not solve the problem of student engagement.

She thought about the big problems the school was facing from the surrounding community. Outside the school, the Truman area of the city had been hit hard by the recent recession, and as the unemployment rate rose, the pressure on the school to serve as a safe haven also rose. The number of students on free and reduced-price lunch had increased 50% since her arrival, and the numbers of families needing language support continued to rise. Meadows knew that she could not address these community problems directly, but students and families brought issues from home into the school, and she and her staff needed to provide the right kinds of support for learners to succeed.

The transportation program, for example, seemed to be working for families involved in the sports programs, but she did not know how the other families felt about the school's transportation efforts. Meadows did know, however, that a group of parents of successful students had started a website to oppose the new inquiry-based science track for students who struggled in math and science. This group of vocal (and influential) Truman parents argued for keeping the existing science program stable as a college-prep pathway for their children. Their concerns made her think about how she and her leadership team could reach out better and include these groups in new efforts moving forward.

Meadows thought that meeting these challenges would require better information about current practices and perspectives in the school. The district press to use data to inform decision making led her to reflect on the information resources she had built with her Truman team. Last year, she persuaded a colleague from her graduate program to join her staff to reform the school data practices. Together they built a strong data system, based on the district data warehouse, to track student progress, disciplinary and placement data, and teacher professional development information. Teachers had access to Google Classroom sites to complement their in-person classrooms; students had access to personal sites to collect and share their work. Meadows thought that if any school in the district had access to the right information to inform planning and progress, it was Truman.

The data the school had collected, however, proved too thin and too removed from practice to guide decision making about strategic priorities. Meadows knew, for example, that the student discipline referral rate had declined in the past year, but she did not know why. It was tempting to attribute the change to the restorative justice program, but she also knew that this was a controversial program and that not all teachers knew about it or how it worked. She knew that the ACT scores had risen slightly over the past two years, but again, she didn't know why. The data they had collected could not tell her team about the effects of their initiatives on the school community or even whether the school community knew about what the leadership team was trying to do in the school.

In her graduate program, several professors had taught about the scientific methods that evaluators use to measure the effects that interventions have had on program outcomes. While these methods excited the research part of her mind, her practical side knew that the controls required for these kinds of methods to be correctly applied could never work in a school like Truman. If experimental design could not fit into the fast-paced world of everyday school leadership and if the data systems she and her team developed could not guide their practice, then how could she get the information she needed to make progress in her school?

It was this inability to connect her practice-based initiatives with results that made her uneasy about her school. So much of what she did every day seemed to be putting out fires—reacting to the problems of other people and developing "good-enough" solutions on the fly. Even when she felt that she and her staff were doing good work, it was difficult to see how their efforts made a difference in how teachers and students interacted every day. With a data system that seemed to focus on the outcomes of the work, she found herself at a loss to think through how she and her team could access the information they needed to understand how their initiatives shaped day-to-day practices and influenced the academic, social, and future lives of Truman students. And if she was struggling with making sense of how practices and results fit together in her school, imagine how leaders new to the field felt or leaders in schools that were failing or beset with resource problems.

What she and her colleagues needed, she thought, *was a map.* A map that could tell educators where they were on the path to improvement and point them in the directions they needed to go. A map of leadership practice.

Distributed Leadership in Action

1

THERE IS NO DOUBT THAT YOU KNOW GOOD LEADERSHIP WHEN YOU SEE IT. The energy in great schools is so palpable that you can feel it the minute you walk into the school.

Throughout our careers, we have worked to understand and capture the dynamics of great school leadership. Having taught in a top-ranked educational leadership preparation program for over 20 years, we have seen many changes in public education, policy, and the expectations of leaders. One of the most exciting and energizing experiences we have had is working in schools with great leaders who strengthen educator capacity and improve learning opportunities for children. We know what creates that energy and what school leaders can do to create the conditions for students, teachers, parents, and staff to engage.

In response to the question, "Who leads?" you might say the principal is the formal, designated leader of the school. After all, the principal is responsible for establishing direction, developing people, and building the capacity of the school organization.[1] The principal sets the tone and ultimately is responsible for the success or failure of the school. A focus on the leadership of the principal is important because a strong principal is critical to the long-term success of the school.

But focusing narrowly on the principal as the leader of the school ignores the many important contributions of others to the nuanced tapestry of leadership that occurs throughout every school day. Consider this sampling from a day in the life of Truman High School:

7:00–7:45 a.m.: The leadership team meets to work on restructuring the school day to create time for teacher teams to collaborate around student work and problems of practice.

7:50–8:00 a.m.: A student confronts one of his peers in the hallway before class and prevents him from bullying another student.

8:00–8:05 a.m.: In morning announcements, the principal welcomes the school community and elicits feelings of school pride as she reminds them what it means to be a Truman Wildcat!

10:00–11:00 a.m.: The math department chair engages math teachers in an examination of data showing that Truman students who fail freshman math are 80 percent less likely to graduate compared to other students. The team plans a strategy to better support students. They agree to examine the data further and determine what areas of freshman math trip up these students the most.

12:00–12:45 p.m.: A paraprofessional works through lunch to help a student struggling in Spanish class.

2:00–2:45 p.m.: A special educator coteaches with the freshman English teacher to ensure that all students can master the core learning outcomes for the course. They plan to share their experiences and mentor other teacher teams during upcoming staff development time.

3:45–4:30 p.m.: The night janitor comes in early to work with the art teacher to clean up a messy student project designed to spark student creativity and expression.

7:00–8:30 p.m.: The choir director supervises a student rehearsal of *The Wiz* as part of her commitment to creating a welcoming space to engage and support students.

Large and small, these and many other regular acts of leadership contribute to shaping Truman's culture of learning.

Understanding the kind of leadership needed in today's educational environment means thinking in a new way about leaders and leadership. Obviously the principal plays a critical leadership role in the school, but the principal's leadership works by engaging and building leadership capacity throughout the school. In other words, the work of leadership is distributed across educators and through tasks that shape the everyday practices of teaching and learning.

LEADERSHIP AND SPAN OF CONTROL

An interesting difference between schools and businesses is that in schools, the span of control—the number of employees a single supervisor oversees—is about *three times* what it is in business. In business today, a typical manager oversees about 10 employees. But in an average elementary school, one leader oversees 33 employees.[2] The span of control is even larger in secondary schools.

In the past, this organizational design wasn't a major problem because leaders were expected to hire good teachers and let them do their jobs. Teachers were considered to be professionals who operated largely on their own. Expectations of teacher autonomy led school leaders to adopt loose, compliance-based practices of supervision and left professional development to the interests of teachers. Teachers taught, and the responsibility—and the consequences—for learning fell on students.

But an interesting shift occurred with implementation of No Child Left Behind in 2002. This law changed the expectations of schools and school leaders. The law required that over a ten-year period, each succeeding class of students needed to produce at higher and higher levels as measured by standardized test scores. The requirement that schools continuously improve scores over time meant that leaders had to continuously build the skills of educators to produce higher and higher levels of achievement. Leaders could no longer simply control hiring and firing; now they were responsible for improving the ability of educators to refine their practices in order to improve outcomes.

Meanwhile, the span of control didn't get any smaller. In support of these improvement expectations, policymakers adopted new curriculum standards, student assessments, evaluation systems, new approaches to special education, and new approaches to student behavior management. These policies provided guidance and resources for schools to improve, but they also required significant time to reevaluate current practices and consider how to best add these new approaches to the daily work of schools.

Even under the old management model, researchers found that principals' days were packed with a series of brief, fragmented interactions with students, parents, teachers, staff, and community members.[3] The new responsibilities for teacher development come on top of managing campus safety, building and grounds, scheduling, public appearances, budget and finance, welcoming visitors, and building a positive climate. Being the principal of a high school is like being a CEO or a mayor of a medium-sized city.

While the federal No Child Left Behind Act has been replaced by the Every Student Succeeds Act, the changes in expectations of schools and school leaders ushered in by No Child Left Behind remain. At the core of the new expectations for school leadership is that leaders can help to improve teaching and learning. Teaching is a complex and uncertain skill. A principal can readily manage the basics of teaching—making sure teachers are in the classroom, on task, maintaining order, covering relevant material, and meeting district or state curriculum and safety requirements. But being responsible for moving teaching practice to the next level requires more than passing through a classroom to make sure everything is all right. It requires intensive engagement with data to understand the dynamics of teaching and learning in the classroom, and making sometimes seemingly small shifts in teaching practice to move learning forward. Most important, it means having the ability to see when teaching is working, when it is not, and knowing what to do to help teachers and learners improve.

LEADER OF LEADERS

In the past, we have thought about leadership as a relationship between leaders and followers. It was the responsibility of the leader to lead and the follower to follow. But we have begun to think about leadership differently. Leadership is not about the relationship between leaders and followers, but the relationship between coleaders and their work.

Schools are service organizations. Anyone who works in a service organization can tell you that the face of the organization is the face of every individual in that organization. When we walk into the bank and talk to the bank teller, he or she is representing the face of that bank. Similarly, when a student has an experience with a teacher in the classroom, that teacher is the face of the school. Because each individual plays such an important role in carrying out the work of the organization, it is important to get everyone on the same page, with the same goals, and the same understandings of how to respond in ways that will move the organization forward. This is a major leadership task for managers in service organizations.

In carrying out the goals of the organization, leadership acts occur all the time and throughout the school. They are carried out by the custodian who makes a connection with a shy student. They are carried out by the school secretary who works with a student to get a message to her parents so she can stay late after school to finish a test. They are carried out by the teacher who seeks feedback and support from other teachers to help him better support student learning. And they are carried out by the student who stands up to confront his peers about a racist remark.

Understanding leadership in this way draws attention away from the role of the leader to the practices that need to be carried out for the school to be effective. It means that the principal doesn't have to have his or her hand in everything that happens in the school. Instead, the principal's role shifts to creating supporting structures and expectations so that many individuals can stand up and take responsibility for carrying out the critical leadership tasks of the school. Mapping leadership means describing how leadership is directed and shared across an organization and guiding the work necessary for effective practice.

DISTRIBUTED LEADERSHIP IN ACTION

The model that principals alone lead schools is outmoded and increasingly irrelevant. Yet many of our ideas to support and evaluate school leadership are still focused on the principal. We need new ways of thinking that take the shared and structural nature of school leadership into account. Distributed leadership theory provides a model for us to map school leadership practice.

Distributed leadership theory began in the late 1990s as a way to think about leadership as a set of tasks directed, shared, and enacted across the school organization. It was initially shaped by pioneering work in distributed cognition. The traditions of cognitive psychology emphasized that understanding thinking depended on studying what went on in the heads of actors. Distributed cognition researchers felt that thinking and acting unfolded in interaction with others and with the environment, and that to think about cognition in terms of the individual alone missed the reality of how cognition unfolds in the world.

In his book *Cognition in the Wild*, Edwin Hutchins analyzed how navigators pilot ships.[4] A central concept in distributed cognition theory is the task, a unit of work that organizes the efforts of actors and is supported (or constrained) by the context of action. While a task can be a novel response to an emergent situation, most tasks are repeated in ways that make work familiar to actors. Over time, repeated tasks help actors form routines that guide action. Learning these routines helps new actors become familiar with how to act and think. For expert actors, routines become the critical resource for how to deal with novelty. Routines become the standard operating procedures for navigational teams to handle ordinary events and react effectively to the extraordinary. Over time, the network of routines forms the organizational culture. The culture becomes a self-defining, and self-preserving, force that bends new initiatives and new actors to expected traditions of the way things are done.

Observing ship navigation led Hutchins to describe two key aspects of how tasks unfold in real work. First, navigation is a social act that involves sharing knowledge through the division of tasks and routines with others. The social nature of thinking in action becomes clear when Hutchins considers the work of navigating a navy amphibious assault ship. "Navigation" is not limited to the work of the officer who has the title. Instead, the actions of navigation are shared by actors across the ship in a complex web of information exchange and decision making. These interactions can take place at the same time (synchronous) or across time (asynchronous) as remembered interactions. Even in a lone outrigger on the Pacific Ocean, remembered conversations about how to use the stars as directional aids are fresh in the practices of the pilot. Thinking in action is always, and irreducibly, social.

Hutchins's second observation is facilitated by the context of action. Navigators rely on a variety of instruments, such as a GPS system, and, in earlier days, sextants and star charts, to guide their work. Without access to these information tools or artifacts, it would be impossible to navigate a ship. Artifacts provide asynchronous guidance to action. Designers build information indicators and knowledge about suggested courses of action into artifacts, such as instruments or policies, that are intended to guide action at some later time to other actors. Of course, some information is typically lost in the distance between the design and the use of such artifacts, which opens up a space for later users to rely on judgment to ascertain the lessons to be drawn from artifacts. Knowing which artifact is appropriate to use when is a key aspect of becoming an expert navigator.

James Spillane and his colleagues adapted key insights from the distributed cognition research to understand the work of school leadership.[5] As with navigation, leadership is concerned with influencing the actions of others. Navigators guide a complex machine—and school leaders engage in a wide variety of tasks to guide the complex mechanisms involved with the social practices of teaching and learning. While teachers engage in the primary work of interacting with students in daily practice, leaders are responsible for providing support, guidance, and resources to ensure that teachers can do their work effectively. When teachers engage in the tasks of organizing work for their colleagues (e.g., through roles such as instructional coaches or department chairs), they too are considered leaders from a distributed perspective. Whoever engages in the work participates in leadership.

The task remains a central concept in distributed leadership. It refers to a unit of work that can be shared across people and supported by the context. Distributed leadership research considers tasks as units of action that constitute practices. Practices refer to how tasks are linked together to form identifiable units of action (e.g., teacher evaluation practices). An important aspect of distributed leadership analysis is to identify the tasks that matter in a given situation.

Distributed leadership, like Hutchins's theory, has two key dimensions. First, leadership is *socially* distributed across the organization. The school principal, of course, is a key actor, but to understand school leadership, we must consider as well the tasks of assistant principals, instructional coaches, special educators, and teachers. These actors sometimes coordinate their work to achieve shared goals, but as often as not, they act independent of one another or even subvert each other's work. The irreducibly political aspects of organizational leadership are shown in how tasks are socially distributed in a school. The tension between leaders and followers is revealed in whether tasks are developed collaboratively with (or imposed on) followers and in whether the intentions of leaders are seen in the actions of followers.

The second dimension of distributed leadership is that it is also *situationally* distributed across the artifacts of the organization. Leaders use tools such as interventions, policies, procedures, and agendas to coordinate tasks in schools. Sometimes they develop these artifacts on their own, but more often they inherit artifacts from the existing structure of the school (like the daily schedule) or must implement artifacts received from outside the school (like a response to intervention program or a district food service contract). Again, the political dimension of leadership is reflected in the situational distribution of practice. Leaders build or advocate programs, such as common planning time or a library maker space, with features designed to support certain kinds of use.

A sign of a strong, shared culture of learning is that teachers and students use such programs as intended. When artifacts are used in ways not intended by designers or in ways that subvert their intended use, this can typically be regarded as an indicator of political or cultural conflict in the school—either because educators and students disagree with the intended uses or because political conflict between leaders is being expressed through subversion. Taken together, the network of artifacts shapes the context of leadership practice in the school. Leaders interested in improving the organization need to add, remove, or redesign tasks to shape a new context of practice.

In order to make space for new directions for action, school leaders must come to understand that school culture is a result of the collective actions of the people, artifacts, and routines that have shaped the current context. Considering culture as a product of tasks, people, artifacts, interactions, and routines shows a pathway for change. Leaders who can identify how the current school culture allows for new action—which educators are open to innovation, for example, and which artifacts are ripe for replacement and renewal—can trace new directions for action. Having a map of existing tasks opens up opportunities to make sustainable change in schools.

TASKS VERSUS SKILLS

Distributed leadership emphasizes the who (leaders) and the what (tasks) of school leadership. But what about the how? What about the personal and interpersonal abilities and skills necessary to persuade followers to join in, or resolve conflicts, or plan for a successful future? Fortunately, researchers have abundantly documented the range of abilities and skills need to successfully lead organizations. Some of these aspects, such as charisma and intelligence, are assumed to be necessary characteristics leaders bring to situations. Other aspects, such as time management, planning, and facilitating social interaction, are described as skills that can be acquired with training and practice. In his influential book *Good to Great*, Jim Collins describes how successful companies have leaders who can assemble high-quality teams, confront hard facts about performance, and focus on what matters to advance the organization.[6] Insights like this have proven inspirational to leaders around the world. Developing these skills and abilities is clearly essential to becoming a successful leader.

If skills are so important, why then does distributed leadership focus on tasks? Distributed leadership research recognizes the abundance of scholarship available on leadership characteristics and also the rich inquiry into how institutional characteristics shape the range of action available to leaders.[7] Because these areas of leadership research are well documented and because books and articles that share these insights are widely available, distributed leadership researchers sought to define a key aspect of practice that was not as well studied—the what of school leadership. As we have seen in our experience as school leadership teachers, developing skills alone does not provide enough guidance to shape successful practice.

In addition to knowing how to communicate and how to focus attention on specific goals, it is also important to know what goals deserve focus. Since every school is unique, yet also shares common features with other schools, the leadership team must be able to ascertain what specific tasks are needed to achieve the larger organizational outcomes. Leaders need to identify, for example, what actions are needed to build professional community in that situation. School leaders need to develop skills and abilities that can, as Jim Collins describes, get the right people on the bus. But determining where that bus should head and which turns it will need to make requires a map that describes the tasks necessary for school improvement.

COMPREHENSIVE ASSESSMENT OF LEADERSHIP FOR LEARNING

Distributed leadership helps make the shift from focusing on the work of individuals to the collection of people, interactions, artifacts, and routines. Mapping these practices and considering how their quality varies according to leadership research and practical experience is the subject of this book.

In 2008, we began our inquiry to map the terrain of leadership practices using the ideas of the distributed leadership framework. We developed rubrics that described leadership at different levels of practice. These rubrics supported our inquiry into helping guide the work of school leaders and identifying areas for improvement. We received a $1.6 million, four-year grant from the U.S. Department of Education to develop and validate a survey that would measure the distributed leadership capacity of a school and provide information to help school leaders improve leadership practices.

To create the survey, we translated the rubrics into a survey of practices. We then gathered focus groups of educators from all levels of K–12 schools over a series of months to identify the ways in which these practices varied across school contexts and to fill in the areas where our rubrics were weak. They helped us capture current practices in schools that struggle, schools that are still developing, and model schools. Our goal was to both capture what we know works and ground it in the experiences of current educators.

The result is the Comprehensive Assessment of Leadership for Learning (CALL), a research-based formative assessment of school leadership practices that invites all educators in a school to provide feedback on the tasks that matter for improving student learning. Between 2011 and 2017, we tested CALL in hundreds of schools with thousands of educators. We developed primary school, secondary school, and district-level versions of CALL and validated the instruments by comparing survey results with measures of school climate, leadership effectiveness, and student learning.

Mapping Leadership tells the story of the leadership work that matters for improving teaching and learning in schools. In most cases, schools use the CALL data formatively to plan local school improvement efforts. In this book, we draw on the incredible information resources provided by thousands of educators to describe the leadership practices that matter in their schools. We begin with a tour of the five key domains of leadership practice: developing a focus on learning, monitoring the practices of teaching and learning, developing professional community, acquiring and allocating resources, and providing a safe and effective learning environment. Each chapter integrates a review of relevant research on the key practices in each domain with the findings of the CALL survey. Each chapter then concludes with directions for the kinds of practices that lead toward improved teaching and learning across schools. We intend this book to be used alone or in conjunction with the CALL survey to support measurement and improvement of distributed leadership practices.[8]

Mapping Leadership aims to provide a bridge between the outcomes that matter and the practices that build the conditions to reach these outcomes. Throughout our careers, we have examined the ways in which leadership is carried out in schools that succeed in improving student learning. We have found that CALL helps educators identify the strengths and weaknesses of their schools and focus attention on critical pathways for school improvement. CALL is the only validated formative assessment of distributed leadership designed to support schools in strengthening their capacity for instructional improvement. We hope you enjoy our tour through what we have learned in our work on the CALL project and that our discussion will spark new directions for how you think about leading your school.

NOTES

1. Leithwood, K., & Riehl, C. (2005).
2. Raiford, S.A. (2004).
3. Peterson, K. D. (1989).
4. Hutchins, E. (1995).
5. See, for example, Spillane, J. P. (2006); Spillane, J. P., Halverson, R., & Diamond, J. B. (2004).
6. Collins, J. (2001).
7. For a review of institutional theory, see Meyer, H. D., & Rowan, B. (2006).
8. Additional information about the survey is available in Appendix A and on our website, www.leadershipforlearning.org.

Mapping School Leadership: Research Base and Domains

MAPPING LEADERSHIP REQUIRES SELECTING THE HIGH-LEVEL DOMAINS of practices that researchers and educators have determined are important to improve teaching and learning in schools and then determining the day-to-day tasks educators perform that enact the key features of these domains. The CALL project has drawn on research findings and extensive interactions with educators to define five domains of leadership practice:

Domain 1: Focus on Learning

Domain 2: Monitoring Teaching and Learning

Domain 3: Building Professional Community

Domain 4: Acquiring and Allocating Resources

Domain 5: Establishing a Safe and Effective Learning Environment

These domains of practice help to define what school leaders can do to establish the conditions to improve teaching and learning in schools. The CALL survey provides a concrete way for schools to measure the degree to which these practices are enacted and describes pathways to coordinate action toward building the capacity for improvement. The result is an action plan that outlines the key tasks a school can take to develop its leadership capacity for school improvement.

KNOWLEDGE BASE FOR THE CALL DOMAINS

Our work to define the tasks that matter for improving leadership for learning was based on two sources: prior research on leadership practices and interactions with a variety of educators. We conducted a thorough review of the leadership for learning research and found key sources that shaped the world of leadership research. Our work draws on these findings and seeks to integrate the insights provided here into the CALL domains of distributed leadership practices. In the next paragraphs, we describe some of the key research findings that provided a significant part of the intellectual foundation for CALL.

First, the Wallace Foundation supported a broad research agenda to describe how effective principals influence school outcomes. This research built on the seminal work of Phillip Hallinger and Ronald Heck, which showed that school leadership is nearly as influential as what happens in classrooms.[1] In 2011, the foundation published a report that summarized the five key responsibilities of leaders for improving schools:[2]

- *Shaping a vision* of academic success for all students, one based on high standards
- *Creating a climate* hospitable to education in order that safety, a cooperative spirit, and other foundations of fruitful interaction prevail
- *Cultivating leadership in others* so that teachers and other adults assume their roles in realizing the school vision
- *Improving instruction* to enable teachers to teach at their best and students to learn to their utmost
- *Managing people, data, and processes* to foster school improvement

Second, the Vanderbilt Assessment of Leadership in Education (VAL-ED) is a widely used survey designed to measure principals' leadership behaviors related to improving student learning. The purpose of the VAL-ED project is to provide ratings for the quality of the principal's practices in a school. The survey invites educators from across a school to provide feedback on the quality of these practices. VAL-ED is organized around the intersection of *core components*, which describe important school characteristics known to influence student learning, and *key processes*, which refer to the work of leaders to shape the six core components, which include:[3]

- High standards for student learning
- Rigorous curriculum
- Quality instruction
- Culture of learning and professional behavior
- Connections to external communities
- Performance accountability

The six key processes are planning, implementing, supporting, advocating, communicating, and monitoring. Together, the intersection of the six core components and six key processes produces 36 scores that rate principal leadership.

Third, Robert Marzano and his colleagues have documented the relation of principals' characteristics and learning outcomes across a wide variety of studies. In his 2005 book, *School Leadership That Works*, Marzano identifies 21 key features of principals' practices that have been correlated with student outcomes.[4] The CALL domains draw on the following features:

- *Change agent*, which describes how the school leader challenges the status quo and pushes toward new practices
- *Cultures of achievement* in the school, which are established and promoted by the leader to guide the work of teaching and learning
- *Discipline*, which describes the responsibility for decreasing the distractions that interfere with instructional time
- *Input*, which measures teachers' influence in running the school, which builds a shared sense of purpose and consensus
- *Involvement in curriculum, instruction, and assessment* practices so that knowledge of strategies and resources can be shared
- *Monitoring/evaluating*, which is important in providing feedback to teachers and students on their learning
- *Order* in routinizing practices so that effort can be focused on improving students' learning
- *Resources* (time, money, supplies, and people) distributed by leaders to shape desired practices

Fourth, the Five Essential Supports developed by Anthony Bryk and his colleagues at the Consortium for Chicago School Research describe the results of over a decade of work to identify the key organizational structures and practices that predict improved learning outcomes in Chicago schools,[5] including:

- *School leadership*, which describes principals who are strategic, focused on instruction, and inclusive of others in their leadership work
- *Parent-community ties*, which describe schools that welcome parents and have strong connections with the community
- *Professional capacity*, which refers to faculty and staff beliefs and values about changing the quality of their professional learning opportunities and their capacity to work together
- *Student-centered learning climate*, which describes the safety of the learning environment
- *Instructional guidance*, which refers to the alignment of the curriculum and learning tools to desired student outcomes[6]

These resources, which summarize a wide variety of research on the relation of school leadership and student outcomes, indicated for us where to dig deeply to uncover the day-to-day actions that foster these high-level practices. The CALL work began where these resources left off. For example, the Wallace and Marzano work mainly described principals' practices. The distributed leadership focus of CALL required reframing these characteristics into work stretched across the school context. The Five Essential Supports identify school leadership as one of the five categories, leaving unspecified how the remaining four categories would come to be in a school context. CALL defines each of the supports as the responsibility of school leaders and describes how schools bring about these conditions in the context of everyday teaching and learning.

Finally, each of these studies relies on the correlation of research constructs to survey results and outcomes as a primary research methodology. The research process typically used in the studies summarized here relies on developing general constructs, such as "monitoring/evaluating" or "parent-community ties" from a selection of survey items. The constructs are then compared with data, such as survey results or school and student outcomes, to determine their importance to predicting student outcomes. The studies confirm that categories such as "quality instruction" are indeed related to student learning outcomes, which is a victory for researchers. However, when it comes to acting on these insights, educators are often left on their own to develop an action plan to make "instructional guidance" or "acting like a change agent" happen in their schools. What counts for research is often not sufficiently formed to guide practices. The devil, and the practice, is often in the details.

CALL DOMAINS OF SCHOOL LEADERSHIP PRACTICE

The CALL map of school leadership practice draws on and extends this rich work to document leadership practices. CALL is organized into a survey of domains, practices, and tasks. The CALL survey has five domains; each domain has three to five practices, each with three to eight tasks. When educators take the CALL survey, each task is represented by an item that defines the tasks and describes an articulation of how each task might be enacted in a school context.

Here we provide an overview of each of the CALL domains needed to make a map of leadership practice. In the following chapters, we visit each domain to discuss the ideas, practices, and day-to-day realities of how leadership can change teaching and learning.

Domain 1: Focus on Learning

1.1　Maintaining a schoolwide focus on learning

1.2　Recognition of formal leaders as instructional leaders

1.3　Collaborative design of integrated learning plan

1.4　Providing appropriate services for students who traditionally struggle

Maintaining a focus on learning means that leaders regularly engage the school community and staff in ongoing conversations to build a collective understanding of the patterns and problems of instruction and student learning. Focus on learning reflects the political and symbolic importance for leaders to establish and maintain a clear direction for the organization and set an example for others by personally engaging in leadership practices. It also describes how leaders act as instructional leaders. School leaders engage in visible instructional leadership activities, such as learning walks or classroom visits, and leaders engage in the professional development activities they design.

Schools that rate highly in Domain 1 have a widely accepted, collaboratively developed, and regularly revisited vision of teaching and learning that reflects the actual practices of school educators. Importantly, the vision of student learning has been translated into an integrated learning plan. Leaders and teachers regularly discuss concrete examples of student work and instructional practice. Special needs staff work together with classroom teachers to plan services for students, and high-quality instructional services are provided in the context of the regular classroom wherever possible.

Domain 2: Monitoring Teaching and Learning

2.1　Formative evaluation of student learning

2.2　Summative evaluation of student learning

2.3　Formative evaluation of teaching

2.4　Summative evaluation of teaching

School leaders are pressed to create and use data to demonstrate the quality of their school program to external audiences and to create data systems for educators to improve their practices. Domain 2 describes how this accountability pressure has resulted in new expectations for leaders to monitor the practices of teaching and learning in order to identify where improvement is needed and create structures to aid educators in improving their work.

Monitoring teaching means creating routines for educators to observe how teaching practices are done and to collect data on the processes and results of teaching. Monitoring learning means collecting data to assess and support the ways in which students are learning. It means establishing practices to document how and where student learning is breaking down, and building routines for educators to review student work and communicate effectively with students about their learning.

In addition to implementing the policies and practices that address accountability pressures, Domain 2 also describes the practices necessary to create a schoolwide information system that educators can use to transform data into effective practices. Monitoring teaching and learning begins in the classroom with the formative evaluation of student learning. We know that formative feedback to students in the classroom is among the most effective tools for improving learning. Leaders must provide structured opportunities for teachers to share and reflect on their practices of providing feedback to students. They must also coordinate interim, or benchmark, assessment practices so that teachers have information about how and whether students are progressing through the curriculum. Interim assessments, delivered through commercial products or self-designed common assessments, provide teachers feedback on student learning goal progress. Teachers carry out much of the work of formative feedback, and leaders are responsible for ensuring a common language and common practices for educators to collect and share formative feedback information across the school in order to create a common vocabulary of instruction.

Educators must also attend to the summative evaluation of student learning. In most schools, this requires leaders to adapt assessment tools, such as standardized tests provided by the state and district, to the instructional culture of the school. They need to help educators make sense of standardized test data by integrating results with other data on student and school performance to provide a more holistic profile of student learning results. Leaders also create regular opportunities for educators to reflect on the results of summative assessments in order to recalibrate the school instructional program.

In schools that rate high in Domain 2, monitoring student learning must be complemented by formative and summative practices to support teachers. Educators must invest time regularly in walk-throughs, classroom visits, or more formal observations to provide meaningful formative feedback to educators. Leaders are responsible for creating fair practices grounded in observation and outcome evidence to summatively evaluate teaching. The summative evaluation process should align with the school's instructional goals and have consequences for improvement or reassignment to noninstructional tasks. Finally, educators align the summative evaluation practices with the school instructional goals and the educator's professional development plan to ensure that everyone is working together toward a common vision for teaching and learning.

CALL is agnostic about a school's chosen instructional ideology. The processes for developing and guiding a schoolwide vision for instruction can be as easily adapted by direct instruction models as by more constructivist, learner-oriented approaches to instruction. From the perspective of school leadership, the important organizational characteristics are the need for collaborative design of a school information culture as a path for staff buy-in and the role that ongoing reflection and data collection play in keeping an instructional vision alive. Focusing on learning for all students also means an increased focus on the needs of students who traditionally struggle the most.

Domain 3: Building Professional Community

3.1   Collaborative schoolwide focus on problems of teaching and learning

3.2   Professional learning

3.3   Socially distributed leadership

3.4   Coaching and mentoring

Researchers and educators agree that building a professional community among educators is at the heart of the school's capacity for improvement. The people in the school are the source of skills, discretion, and knowledge required to effectively teach students and interact with the school community. Professional community requires educators to work together to share instructional strategies and risk experimenting with new practices in order to collectively improve. Leaders must create professional environments in which educators trust one another enough to take risks, learn, problem-solve, and share new practices together.

A number of tasks indicate the quality of a school's professional community. First, leaders seek to build instructional program coherence by recognizing that any efforts for change are built on existing professional practices. Professional community relies on a common context for practice. Effective leaders do not simply pile new initiatives on top of last year's efforts. Instead, they work with educators to make sense of the new in terms of the old to build instructional program coherence. Professional development, curriculum design, and school improvement are designed to reflect this collective sense-making effort.

The resilience of a professional community depends on the quality of the staff learning opportunities. As professionals and lifelong learners, educators are responsible for pursuing their own learning goals. The work of school leaders is to establish the resources and the direction to coordinate learning interests toward shared instructional goals. In what ways has the school developed a long-term plan for both individual and shared professional learning to meet key instructional priorities? Leaders design workshops and professional development sessions and make use of new media to create opportunities for educators to learn on their own time. Leaders are responsible for establishing practices to measure the results of professional learning in terms of changes in teaching practices and improvement in student learning.

Professional communities depend on sharing information among staff with different abilities and experience. Leaders create meaningful opportunities for mentoring and coaching among staff. For example, are mentor teachers chosen based on their knowledge, skills, and abilities to work with colleagues? Is the influence of instructional coaches localized among small groups of educators or felt throughout the school?

Robust professional communities blur the distinctions between leaders and followers by encouraging broad participation in decision making and leadership activities. A distributed leadership framework captures this movement from educator (i.e., interacting with students for learning) to leader (i.e., establishing the conditions of practice for educators). It is important to attend to how leaders structure opportunities for educators to develop and implement instructional initiatives in the school and provide processes to collect feedback on new programs and budget priorities. An important pathway for building professional community is when educators collaboratively design the instructional program of the school.

Domain 4: Acquiring and Allocating Resources

4.1 Personnel practices

4.2 Structuring and maintaining time

4.3 School resources focus on student learning

4.4 Integrating external expertise into the school instructional program

4.5 Coordinating and supervising relations with families and external communities

Using resources to support school goals is an important part of leadership. Leaders need to be able to access new sources of materials and time and to reorganize existing resources to meet new instructional needs. In schools that score highly in Domain 4, leaders hire teachers with the skills needed to meet student learning needs and support those new teachers in building mentoring and peer networks to succeed. Leaders organize time for instructional improvement and teacher collaboration. CALL asks how much time is provided for whole school, grade-level, and subject matter reflection and how students are assigned to instructional resources. Schools also live in a wider network of community and knowledge resources. CALL explores how well schools use external experts, including district and external consultants, to provide support for school improvement. The work of external experts needs to be designed to support the vision of teaching and learning. Leaders must also coordinate and supervise processes to link families into the school community.

Domain 5: Establishing a Safe and Effective Learning Environment

5.1 Clear, consistent, and enforced expectations of student behavior

5.2 Clean and safe learning environment

5.3 Support services for students who traditionally struggle

A safe and effective learning environment is the foundation for educators and students to take the chances needed to engage in learning. This means more than discouraging negative behaviors: leaders must establish a positive learning environment that encourages risk taking, experimentation, and learning from failure among educators and students. CALL articulates the tasks associated with creating a safe learning environment for students, such as communicating clear, consistent, and enforced expectations for student behavior; creating clean and safe spaces for learning; and developing safe havens for all students. Leaders also need to buffer teachers from interruptions to classroom instruction by facilitating interactions with parents and community members while creating a welcoming atmosphere in which visitors can participate in the school community. In Domain 5, CALL also examines the presence of key practices such as response to intervention and positive behavioral intervention systems.

THE CALL SURVEY IN ACTION

The CALL survey measures each of these practices with questions designed to measure the tasks that matter. The levels of practice were developed based on research on schools and refined by educators to reflect their experiences of low to high levels of practice. The survey has been administered in over 600 urban, suburban, and rural contexts across the United States and internationally. Schools and districts administer the survey to measure distributed leadership and provide formative feedback on leadership practices for school improvement.

The CALL survey development began by using research to identify the key domains of practices, then translated these practices into items that describe the everyday work of educators. The CALL work began with two sets of rubrics we developed to describe leadership practices at different levels of action.[7] These rubrics relied heavily on our literature review and sought to describe the ways that educators could engage with these practices. Comparing our initial rubrics with the research base led us to frame the five CALL domains and translate the rubrics into survey items for educators to rate themselves.

As the CALL project got under way, we brought together groups of experts and career educators—teachers, principals, coordinators, coaches, district leaders, and specialists—to articulate the necessary work involved with achieving the goals of each domain, then to specify the range of desired practice in the structure of each. This led us to consider the role of formative feedback in developing a survey of practice. Leadership surveys typically assess perceptions about the degree to which an item describes reality. For example, an educator might be asked to respond to an item like this:

My principal leads by example:

Strongly Disagree   Disagree   Agree   Strongly Agree

We found that these types of questions may be valuable for rating a principal, but they provide little information on how to improve practice. Our educator focus groups shared their concern that most of the surveys they took or invited students to take seemed obsessed with rating but did not provide enough information to do anything about the rating. We decided that the CALL survey would be different: the range of answers for each item would describe the range of practices that characterized that task. In other words, each item would itself provide a form of formative feedback—a map of possible action—that could guide a community from one level of practice to the next.

The following example uses an item about how leaders coordinate English language learning (ELL) practices in the school. The CALL item reads:

In most classes in your school, who is <u>primarily</u> responsible for teaching English language learners or ELL students?

- No one takes primary responsibility for teaching these students.
- The English language learner teacher.
- The English language learner teacher <u>and</u> the classroom teacher, but the <u>English language learner</u> teacher develops the learning plans.
- The English language learner teacher <u>and</u> the classroom teacher, but the <u>classroom teacher</u> develops the learning plans.
- The English language learner teacher, the classroom teacher, and support team work together to develop the learning plans.

The item has several goals built into the question. First, the item indicates that coordinating the practices of English language teachers and learners is an important leadership task. Second, the item options describe an articulation of desired practices. In schools without specified support, ELL students do not receive extra help (or there may not be ELL students in the school). In schools with ELL supports, the research on inclusive practices suggests that ELL students learn best when the classroom teachers share responsibility for the student's learning (instead of, for example, simply allowing the ELL teacher to guide learning). Building the research base into the item options allows educators not only to rate their own practices but also to see what the next level of practice might look like and plan for improvement in terms of the item options.

After extensive discussions with educators and testing the survey in schools across the country, we decided that this approach to using a leadership survey as a formative feedback instrument for school planning held potential for helping schools improve their practices. The domains of the CALL survey begin with the research in school leadership practices, but the need to specify each task down to classroom practice means that the knowledge needed to inform the item design stretched far beyond the domain of traditional leadership work into areas such as school-community relations, special education, data-driven decision making, formative feedback, accountability policies, restorative justice, strategic planning, and many more areas relevant to the day-to-day practices of school improvement.

Of course, the practices selected for the CALL survey are not an exhaustive representation of what leaders do. There are many, many tasks for educators to establish the conditions for teaching and learning. Some of these practices, such as community outreach and participation in extracurricular events and civic organizations, are related to responding to the political conditions of schools. Other tasks include complying with state and national requirements in such areas as budget reporting, student records, and special education. Many schools are engaged in specific reform efforts, such as International Baccalaureate, community schools, or personalized learning, that require further leadership work. Describing the work of leaders is surely as endless as it feels for educators in the midst of keeping their schools rolling.

Mapping the full range of practices may well impress observers with the extraordinary range of what school leaders do to manage schools. But a map is not the same as a terrain. A map narrows information to provide a useful guide for the features of the terrain that matter for navigation. CALL selects from the relevant research and expert perspectives to cull a set of practices necessary for the work of improving learning in schools. In the chapters that follow, we present each of the CALL domains and highlight the specific research and practices that led us to conclude that this work matters to improving teaching and learning in schools.

NOTES

1. Hallinger, P., & Heck, R. H. (1998).
2. Wallace Foundation. (2011).
3. Porter, A., Murphy, J., Goldring, E., Elliot, S., Polikoff, M. S., & May, H. (2008).
4. Marzano, R. J. (2005).
5. Bryk, A. S., Sebring, P. B., Allensworth, E., Luppescu, S., & Easton, J. Q. (2010).
6. Consortium for Chicago School Research. (2012).
7. Halverson's rubrics resulted from a fruitful collaboration from 2004 to 2006 with the University of Pittsburgh's Institute for Learning (http://ifl.pitt.edu). Kelley's rubrics were described in her 2009 book with Jim Shaw, *Learning first! A School Leader's Guide to Closing Achievement Gaps.*

Domain 1: Focus on Learning

| | 1 Focus on Learning | | 2 Monitoring Teaching & Learning | | 3 Professional Community | | 4 Acquiring & Allocating Resources | | 5 Safe & Effective Environment |

DOMAIN 1: FOCUS ON LEARNING	TOTAL	ELEMENTARY	SECONDARY	LEADERS
	3.6	**3.6**	**3.6**	**3.8**
1.1 Maintaining a schoolwide focus on learning	3.5	3.6	3.5	3.9
1.2 Recognition of formal leaders as instructional leaders	3.8	3.8	3.7	4.1
1.3 Collaborative design of integrated learning plan	3.5	3.5	3.5	3.8
1.4 Providing appropriate services for students who traditionally struggle	3.6	3.6	3.6	3.5

Note: Five-point scale. $N = 18{,}677$ respondents.

3

Domain 1: Focus on Learning

	3.8	3.8	3.9	3.9
1.1 Maintaining a schoolwide focus on learning	3.5	3.6	3.6	3.8
1.2 Recognition of formal teachers as instructional leaders	3.6	3.6	3.7	4.1
1.3 Collaborative design of integrated learning plan	3.5	3.5	3.5	3.8
1.4 Providing appropriate services for students who traditionally struggle	3.5	3.6	3.6	3.5

Note. Five-point scale. N = 18172 respondents.

ALL SCHOOLS HAVE STORIES TO TELL. EVERY PERSON WHO WORKS AND studies in the school lives this story. Each person's life is a sequence of experiences that can be drawn into a narrative to make sense of what comes next on the basis of what has gone before. The patterns that emerge across these stories come to form the story of the school. In schools that have met big challenges, staff and students face novelty with confidence; in schools with a narrative of struggle, teachers and staff shrug off the possibility of positive change. These primary narratives bring together the perceptions of the defining routines of the school with the central challenges that the community faces.

From a leadership perspective, these stories become an opportunity to shape the identity of the school. In *Leading Minds: An Anatomy of Leadership*, Howard Gardner posits that the leader's impact "depends most significantly on the particular story that he or she relates or embodies."[1] Leaders "tell stories . . . about themselves and their groups, about where they are headed, about what was to be feared, struggled against, and dreamed about." Traditional leaders tell stories that fit with and reinforce the dominant themes of the existing stories. Transformational leaders tell stories that extend, reverse, or complement the existing stories with new narratives that persuade the audience to move in new directions. If the new story is too radical, the culture will likely reject the leader; if the new story is too conventional, the community will have difficulty rallying around change.

Of course, everyone recognizes the story that schools are for learning. Teachers teach so that students learn and schools are organized to maximize student-teacher interaction. But schools have many other stories to tell. Schools are social service providers, sources of guidance and inspiration (and boredom), contested political spaces, and places of work. These stories exist alongside one another in the culture of most schools, contesting for space in the stories of teachers and learners. Instructional leaders need to give voice to the "school as a place of learning" story in ways that make sense to the community and create space for new practices.

The first CALL domain describes how leaders tell and live a story that focuses the school community on learning. Successful leaders in Domain 1 say that learning is important, and they live the focus on learning in their day-to-day actions. What does it mean to tell a story that focuses on learning? Gardner's work emphasizes the role of the formal leader in telling and living the story. While a distributed leadership perspective emphasizes the work done by actors across the school, the practices in Domain 1 emphasize how the formal leader, typically the principal, lives the story of a focus on learning. Traditionally, this work is described in terms of the principal as instructional leader.[2] The principal must live a model that teaching and learning are important and must set up (and participate in) structures that support a focus on learning throughout the school. Setting this example draws out the mission of focusing on student learning that rallies community members around a common mission.

Domain 1: Focus on Learning has been identified as an important component of principals' leadership for some time. Defined as instructional leadership, this ability to narrow the diversity of school narratives to a focus on learning was identified as a key aspect of effective leadership in high-performing urban schools.[3] The professional standards for school leaders were designed to emphasize instructional leadership to guide the preparation, professional development, and evaluation of principals. The No Child Left Behind law reinforced instructional leadership by holding leaders accountable for improving state test scores for all students, as well as for subgroups disaggregated by race, income, language, and special education status. Mary Canole and Michelle Young noted that "by 2005, 46 states had adopted or slightly adapted the standards, or had relied upon them to develop their own set of state standards," thus providing legislative and regulatory accountability for principals' leadership focused on learning.[4]

Our approach to describing the CALL domains and practices is to highlight the tasks involved with enacting these practices, then to use the data from the CALL survey to illustrate patterns in how these tasks are done in schools across the country. Four subdomains make up the Focus on Learning:

SUBDOMAIN	CORE PRACTICES
1.1 Maintaining a schoolwide focus on learning	Leaders tell and live a story that demonstrates a shared mission that focuses on student learning.
1.2 Recognition of formal leaders as instructional leaders	Leaders allocate time to symbolically demonstrate commitment to a focus on improving teaching and learning.
1.3 Collaborative design of integrated learning plan	School processes are guided by a common plan that focuses professional development and instructional improvement.
1.4 Providing appropriate services for students who traditionally struggle	Classroom and special needs teachers work together to create meaningfully inclusive learning environments for all students.

1.1 MAINTAINING A SCHOOLWIDE FOCUS ON LEARNING

- Do leaders tell a story of a school focused on learning?
- Are there regular opportunities to share this story with educators and the community?
- Is there a common language of instruction across the school?

A schoolwide vision focused on student learning and shared by all members of the school community is characteristic of schools that close achievement gaps and improve learning for all students. Pursuit of the vision provides clear guidance for action, a shared identity for the school community, and a safe space for collective problem solving as all members of the school work to achieve the same goals.

These practices have become part of the DNA of leadership practice in the United States. According to the CALL survey data, ninety percent of elementary school teachers and administrators and 86% of middle and high school teachers and administrators report that at least every semester, school leaders engage each staff member in conversations to build a shared vision of student learning in the school. Furthermore, 57% of elementary school staff and 48% of middle and high school staff report that they engage in these conversations at least monthly.

Analysis of data is a core feature of high-performing schools. Communicating the priority of data-driven cultures is a key aspect of contemporary instructional leadership. (We have more to say about the specific practices of data-driven leadership in Chapter 4.) Leadership in these schools creates opportunities to collect, acquire, and store data; reflect and set goals based on the data; create interventions; and develop practices to learn from the data. Halverson and colleagues document the presence of these data-driven instructional systems in schools and highlight the importance of these systems in fostering shared understanding and direction.[5] The distributed nature of leadership in schools, norms of professional autonomy, and the physical structure of schools (typically one teacher in one classroom with many students, with limited opportunities for interaction with other teachers during the workday) create challenges to building shared understanding and commitment to reform.

The uses of data in schools parallel the diversity of narratives. Teachers and students interpret new information on the basis of the stories they use to make sense of their experiences in school. As a result, the novel opportunities for action are often explained away in current norms and practices.[6] Curating information that disconfirms the current story can open up new perspectives for interpretation. Through structured and focused discussions of student achievement data, grades, and grading practices, school leaders can create opportunities to question the existing stories and create shared commitment around new narratives. Using data can open opportunities to solve rather than to explain difficult problems of practice that in turn generate an emergent shared identity.[7]

As we shall see in Chapter 5, data should open up opportunities for designs that build shared understandings, promote relational trust, and build and maintain commitment to a course of action to address gaps between the current state and the school's goals. Leaders should give voice to the importance of frequent conversations that facilitate the development of a common language of instruction. These interactions between and among teachers should not be left to chance; they should include formal time set aside for teacher conversations. They should have a clear agenda and follow principles of effective meeting processes.

The CALL data testify to the frequency of these kinds of agenda-setting practices.

- Eighty-three percent of elementary teachers and 73% of secondary teachers indicated that their administrators set up formal meeting times to discuss student achievement data at least once a semester, with 43% of elementary teachers and 33% of secondary teachers reporting meeting at least monthly.

- About 70% of both elementary and secondary teachers indicated that their administrators set up formal meeting times for them to discuss student grades at least once a semester.

- Nearly one in five teachers at both the elementary and secondary levels reported that they never held these conversations.

Teacher collaboration time can lack clarity in focus, and teachers don't always participate in collaborative conversations about teaching and learning. This may help to explain why administrators reported much higher rates of formally scheduled time for teachers to discuss grades, with about 75% of elementary school administrators and 82% of secondary school administrators reporting that they scheduled time for teachers to meet to discuss student grades at least once a semester.

Discussing grading practices is a valuable way to segue into discussing current practice. Many schools have grading practices that provide consistent signals of student learning related to curriculum standards. A substantial number of teachers report that they have regularly scheduled meetings with other teachers to discuss grading practices. Seventy percent of elementary and secondary school teachers report that their school administrators schedule formal meetings to discuss grading practices at least once a semester.

An important outcome of a shared focus on learning is a common language to describe instructional practices. A common language is evidence that teachers have had deep and meaningful conversations about instruction, enough to develop shared understandings of what instruction looks like. Having a common understanding of language about instruction facilitates additional conversations and opportunities for continuous improvement of instructional practices:

- About 85% of teachers report that they share a common language of instruction.

- A shared language of instruction is more common across subject areas (just over half of high school teachers and 63% of elementary school teachers) than it is within subject areas (33% of high schools teachers and 21% of elementary school teachers).

- Only about 3% of teachers say they never talk to their colleagues about instruction. Another 12% report that they talk about instruction but do not share a common language about instructional practices, suggesting that the depth or frequency of these conversations may be limited.

Our data suggest that most schools have structured time in place for meaningful conversations to build shared understandings of the goals for teaching and learning. However, one in four teachers does not have scheduled time to talk about student learning data, grades, or grading practices with their colleagues at least once a semester. This suggests that leaders can provide more opportunities to analyze data and build a shared commitment and direction to improving student learning. Schools that have structures in place to promote conversations among teachers about teaching and learning have developed shared understandings about instructional practices within and often across subject areas.

1.2 RECOGNITION OF FORMAL LEADERS AS INSTRUCTIONAL LEADERS

- Do leaders model active and engaged participation in professional learning?
- Do leaders set a clear vision for teaching and learning?
- Are teachers held accountable for high levels of performance?

Research suggests that schools recognize a focus on learning when principals engage in symbolic leadership.[8] The principal is the formal leader in many schools. Although CALL uses a distributed leadership model, the principal still plays a symbolic role central to the community. Principals lead symbolically by publicly explaining how initiatives and decisions about resource allocation fit with the school's instructional vision. They model active participation in school improvement through their own meaningful participation, relating a clear and consistent story of effective teaching and high-level learning for all students, and holding themselves and others accountable for high-quality student learning outcomes. In larger schools, some responsibilities of the principal may be delegated to members of the leadership team, but the principal still needs to tell the story of instructional leadership to consistently prioritize the importance of these activities.

Symbolic leadership involves communicating through direct actions (e.g., storytelling, ceremonies) and indirect actions that are embedded in daily routines (e.g., resource allocation, attendance, and participation in events).[9] The symbolic work of the principal focuses teacher attention on the school mission. Of course, leaders can speak to serve one message but act to satisfy another. Symbolic leadership requires that formal leaders understand that their position invites inspection. When leaders act in conflict with the organization story, they undermine the potential of a shared narrative. Leader actions cue followers for what counts as a priority in an organizational context.

Our teachers report that about 70% of principals take an active, participatory role alongside teachers in schoolwide learning activities. Too little engagement by the principal may be as detrimental as too much, as principals may either fail to engage in activities, signaling that they don't believe they are important, or take over the activities, diminishing teacher agency. Only 8% of teachers perceive that principals err by taking over professional development activities, while nearly a quarter of principals fail to engage in professional development activities.

Principals communicate their priorities by the ways in which they spend their time. Among the instructional activities we measured, leaders prioritize setting a clear vision for teaching and learning the most, with 86% of administrators at all school levels indicating that this is a very important or extremely important priority. While the teacher ratings are slightly lower, 71% of secondary school teachers and 75% of elementary school teachers report that this is a priority for their administrators.

Principals in CALL schools emphasized the importance of accountability in their school narratives.[10] Eighty-two percent of secondary school leaders and 85% of elementary school leaders report that holding educators (including themselves) accountable for teaching and learning is an important priority. Teachers generally agree, with 69% of secondary school teachers and 77% of elementary teachers reporting that their administrators prioritize accountability for teaching and learning as very or extremely important.

While principals are very engaged in symbolic practices to signify the importance of teaching and learning, there is significant disagreement between leaders and educators about how principals are engaged in the actual work of helping teachers improve their practice:

- According to teacher ratings, elementary school principals (60%) are more engaged than secondary school principals (51%) in working with teachers individually to improve practice.

- Administrator ratings indicate that 75% of elementary principals and 73% of secondary principals prioritize working individually with teachers to improve their teaching practice.

- About 20% of teachers report that school leaders never engage in classroom visits or learning walks to improve instruction.

- Administrators report higher levels of participation than teachers; nevertheless, only about 40% of administrators report that they participate in classroom visits or learning walks one or more times per week.

Administrators may not engage in more hands-on activities to promote instructional improvement for a variety of reasons. One is that leaders have too many role demands that impede their ability to focus on instruction. The Wallace

Foundation School Administration Manager project focused on developing a new role in schools that would free up principal time to focus on instructional leadership. This research found that principals spend 32% of their time on instruction-related activities. Through the addition of a second administrative manager role in the school and with training to support reflective leadership practice focused on teaching and learning, principals participating in the Wallace Foundation project were able to increase the amount of their time spent on instruction to an average of 45%.[11]

While our analysis does not measure specific time commitments, it does examine the extent to which principals and teachers view instructional leadership as a priority. Our data suggest that these types of individually focused practices are prioritized lower, and carried out less frequently, than broader schoolwide instructional leadership activities that have been shown to have less impact on instructional improvement.

1.3 COLLABORATIVE DESIGN OF INTEGRATED LEARNING PLAN

- Is there a formal schoolwide process that enables teachers to collaborate to improve instruction?
- Do leaders regularly schedule time for teachers to discuss strategies for instruction?
- Is an action plan or school improvement plan in use that improves student learning?
- Is schoolwide professional development designed to advance school goals and meet each teacher's learning needs?

Because the time for school leaders and instructional staff to collaborate is limited, creating meeting time that is meaningful, focused, and rewarding is critical to effective instructional design. The next set of leadership practices focuses on providing time for teachers to work together around issues of instruction and school improvement. This section of CALL describes how leaders create the space to allow for meaningful professional interaction. (Chapter 5 discusses how this space for learning can be transformed into a powerful professional learning community.)

The practice of building a school improvement plan emerged as a best practice in the effective schools research.[12] The school improvement plan is particularly useful in establishing shared understandings of current conditions and plans for action and in helping to align individual agents operating in a distributed system.

School improvement planning is one of the most common collaborative design processes in schools. Engaging in planning helps teachers and staff to develop a shared understanding of school goals; it can also help build commitment to strategies for improvement. School improvement plans are a critical element of shared sense making and commitment. More than one in 10 educators in the CALL survey reported that their school has no school improvement planning process. The vast majority of teachers report that their schools are developing or have a school improvement plan, but only one in four elementary school teachers and one in five secondary school teachers report that their school improvement planning process actually succeeds in improving student learning.

Another important shared sense-making activity is collaborative work to improve instructional practice. Leaders are responsible for creating opportunities for teachers to plan together. Sixty-eight percent of elementary teachers and 93% of secondary teachers report that their principal has created at least monthly opportunities to meet and discuss instruction. Taking advantage of these opportunities for collaborative design varies widely in schools:

- Seven percent of educators report that they create plans to improve instruction on their own.
- Twenty-six percent report that they voluntarily collaborate with other teachers to develop plans to improve instruction.
- Twenty-eight percent of teachers report that they work in schools where almost all teachers participate in formal collaborative activities to improve instruction.

These data suggest that more formal opportunities are needed for teachers to work together to improve instruction. But they also suggest that when formal opportunities are created, the teachers often do not take advantage of that time to work together. As we explore in Chapter 5, the norms of collaborative work need to be established early, clear agendas need to be developed for teacher team meetings, and teachers need to be held accountable for their time working together. Educators may lack the skills or the authority to take leadership roles in leading critical conversations about instruction with colleagues. Our data suggest that even when principals take an active management role in creating occasions for interaction, there is still work to be done in helping educators to realize the potential of these opportunities.

School leaders signal the focus and importance of teacher learning through the design of schoolwide professional development activities. Data from the CALL study reflect research that finds schoolwide professional development is often of low quality and fails to advance teacher learning.[13] Twenty-five percent of teachers reported that professional development does not reflect the instructional goals of the school and does not address their learning needs. Only 18% of elementary school teachers and 21% of middle and high school teachers report that schoolwide professional development is designed in ways that recognize and build on existing teacher expertise.

1.4 PROVIDING APPROPRIATE SERVICES FOR STUDENTS WHO TRADITIONALLY STRUGGLE

- Is the school proactive in preventing student failure?
- Do classroom teachers take ownership for the learning of all students?
- Do all students receive differentiated instruction in the regular classroom?
- Do classroom and special needs teachers collaborate to develop instruction for all students?

Public schools need to attend to the learning of all students. Leaders need to use policy tools to build systems that can identify and support student learning. In Chapter 7, we examine the tools at hand, such as response to intervention, positive behavioral intervention supports, and restorative justice initiatives, to build systems of support. In this section, we discuss the story that leaders need and the symbolic actions they take to ensure that all children have an equal opportunity to learn.

In equitable schools, leaders emphasize the role of teachers to anticipate the learning needs of all students and provide motivation, engagement, and instructional designs that enable everyone to succeed. Educators collaborate to ensure that they are aware of changes in student academic performance or behavior that may reflect an underlying problem that needs to be addressed to enable students to succeed. All teachers take responsibility for the learning of all students and develop instructional strategies designed to promote learning and prevent failure.

The expectation is that the learning needs of all students are met in inclusive classrooms in the least restrictive environment and that all teachers differentiate instruction and provide scaffolding and support as a fully integrated part of their practice. The message in equitable schools is that supporting the success of all students means identifying barriers to learning early so that they can be addressed long before a student receives a failing grade in a class. Meeting with students, parents, and staff to discuss learning issues and working to resolve them provides scaffolding to support student success. Telling the story of equitable schooling sets the expectation that the mission of the school is to provide a high-quality education for all students.

The CALL survey provides interesting data on how widely the story of equity is told and lived in schools. For the issue of educators taking responsibility for the learning of all students, the CALL data report the following findings:

- For students with specific learning disabilities, both elementary and secondary school teachers report that the special education teacher is primarily responsible for instruction about 25% of the time.

- About 33% of teachers report that classroom and special education teachers effectively collaborate in the design and delivery of instruction for students with specific learning disabilities.

- Twenty-seven percent of teachers report that they don't know who is responsible for teaching English language learners, and another 10% report that in their school, no one takes primary responsibility for teaching these students.

- Twenty-two percent of elementary teachers and 17% of secondary teachers report that classroom and English language learner teachers effectively collaborate in the design and delivery of instruction for nonnative-English speaking students.

Ideally, special education students would be integrated into the regular classroom, and both the regular and special education teachers would take on primary responsibility for the learning of students with special learning needs. While most schools promote equitable learning opportunities, the CALL data help us to understand the variation on how these opportunities are reflected in day-to-day practices.

Research suggests that students learn best when they are placed in the regular classroom rather than being segregated into a special needs classroom.[14] The CALL survey measures teacher perceptions of whether students with special learning needs are taught in pullout programs or regular classrooms; whether students have customized services to support their learning needs; and whether classrooms are effectively differentiated to support diverse learners. Table 3.1 presents the CALL data on these key practices of supporting the needs of diverse learners.

Table 3.1 shows that a significant number of students are still taught in segregated, pullout classrooms or classrooms without accommodations in CALL schools. Only about a third of teachers report an ideal scenario: that students with special needs are taught in the regular classroom with effective differentiated instruction for all students.

While the majority of students with special learning needs receive instruction in the regular classroom that is effectively differentiated for all students, a very large minority of students still spend significant time in pullout programs or

Table 3.1 Key Practices for Supporting the Needs of Diverse Learners in Elementary and Secondary Schools

		EXCLUDED FROM CLASSROOM IN PULLOUT PROGRAMS	REGULAR CLASS-ROOMS OR NO ACCOM-MODATION	IN REGULAR CLASS-ROOMS, INCLUDED IN THE REGULAR LESSON	IN REGULAR CLASSROOMS WITH DIFFERENTIATION
Learning	ES	29%	9%	26%	36%
disabilities	SS	6	9	46	39
Emotional/	ES	13	16	38	33
behavioral disabilities	SS	11	13	47	29
Cognitive	ES	31	12	24	33
disabilities	SS	27	13	31	29
English language	ES	15	13	34	38
learners	SS	7	15	45	32
Gifted	ES	15	15	30	40
and talented	SS	6	16	40	38

Note: ES: elementary schools; SS: middle and high schools. $N = 10,274$.

regular classrooms without accommodation. Our data suggest that significantly more attention needs to be paid to the structure of student time. Research is clear that pullout programs do not improve learning for students, yet large proportions of students with special learning needs continue to be removed from the classroom for their instruction. Despite research evidence suggesting that students learn best when they are in inclusive environments, there is still a heavy emphasis on pullout programs, and teachers in the classroom do not always carry out best instructional practices to address the needs of diverse learners. The structural elements of these changes are relatively easy to fix, but changing school cultures around teacher and student time can be challenging politically. This requires attention to data and the development of strong shared commitment to change.

We return to this topic in Chapter 7, where we discuss the ways in which contemporary approaches to services for students who struggle overlap with demands to create a safe learning environment.

PUTTING IT ALL TOGETHER TO FOCUS ON LEARNING

Mapping leadership requires us to describe how leaders set the tone for educators to pick out the theme of student learning as the essential goal. Leaders need to tell, and live, the story of how focusing on learning will satisfy the professional aspirations for educators and address what all students need at school.

CALL Domain 1 focuses on the actions that the principal and other school leaders take to create the structures, cultures, and supports to generate shared understandings and align and motivate action. Our data suggest that leaders engage with staff in collaborative conversations about teaching and learning that enable schools to create shared understandings about student learning needs and effective teaching practice, which are facilitated by the development of a shared language to describe instructional practice.

Four leadership practices in Domain 1 are key:

- *Building community around learning:* Leaders build the capacity for teachers and staff to foster a shared commitment to improving student learning.
- *Telling and living the story:* Principals talk and act in ways that demonstrate a commitment to the story of the school's focus on learning.

- *Engaging the community in planning:* Leaders design processes that involve the schoolwide community in the design of strategic and instructional improvement plans.
- *Focusing on equity:* Inclusive learning environments are created for all students.

Domain 1 shows that the symbolic and modeling work of school leaders to tell the story of a focus on student learning is widely embraced across CALL schools. Most CALL leaders are perceived as successful in creating structures that support teacher engagement in improving teaching and learning. They structure time during the school year for teachers to collaborate to improve instruction. In the vast majority of schools, a school improvement plan is actively used and improves student learning, and there are schoolwide professional development activities designed to advance school goals and meet each teacher's learning needs.

We found mixed evidence, however, that schools are consistently implementing best practices in supporting students who struggle in the regular classroom. The mission to produce equitable outcomes and equal access to learning opportunities continues to challenge our public school leaders and educators. The work of providing equitable learning opportunities and outcomes moves beyond setting the stage and telling a story of focusing on learning. It requires specific practices for building information systems that provide feedback to teachers and learners, building resilient professional learning communities, acquiring and allocating resources that support equitable practices, and building safe learning environments. In the next chapters, we map these dimensions of the kinds of work required to improve student and teacher practices throughout the school—the work that enacts a focus on learning for all students.

NOTES

1. Gardner, H. (1995).
2. Recent research by Jason Grissom, Susanna Loeb, and Ben Master calls the traditional model of principal-involved-in-the-classroom into question. Their work shows that this type of principal time is negatively correlated with student achievement. This does not mean, however, that leaders should ignore what happens in the classroom. Instead, Grissom, Loeb, and Master (2013) emphasize the positive influences of support for teacher collaboration and instructional coaching on student outcomes. From a distributed leadership perspective, the work of leaders is to promote a schoolwide focus on learning across the school, not just the work of the formal leaders.
3. Hallinger, P. (1992); Lezotte, L. W., & Snyder, K. M. (2011).

4. Canole, M., & Young, M. (2013).
5. Halverson, R., Grigg, J., Prichett, R., & Thomas, C. (2007).
6. Bolman, L. G., & Deal, T. E. (2008).
7. Wenger, E. (1998).
8. Deal, T. E., & Peterson, K. D. (1994); Reitzug, U. C., & Reeves, J. E. (1992).
9. Reitzug, U. C. (1994).
10. Elmore, R. F., & Fuhrman, S. H. (2001).
11. Turnbull, B. J., Haslam, M. B., Arcaira, E. R., Riley, D. L., Sinclair, B., & Coleman, S. (2009).
12. Lezotte, L. W., & Jacoby, B. C. (1990).
13. For a review on the effects of professional development on learning, see Yoon, K. S., Duncan, T., Lee, S. W.-Y., Scarloss, B., & Shapley, K. (2007).
14. Baker, E. T. (1995).

Domain 2: Monitoring Teaching and Learning

DOMAIN 2: MONITORING TEACHING AND LEARNING	TOTAL	ELEMENTARY	SECONDARY	LEADERS
	3.3	**3.4**	**3.2**	**3.3**
2.1 Formative evaluation of student learning	3.6	3.7	3.6	3.5
2.2 Summative evaluation of student learning	3.5	3.6	3.4	3.5
2.3 Formative evaluation of teaching	2.7	2.7	2.7	3.0
2.4 Summative evaluation of teaching	3.3	3.4	3.2	3.6

Note: Five-point scale. $N = 18,677$ respondents.

MONITORING INSTRUCTION HAS BECOME A MORE SUBSTANTIVE PART of school leadership in recent years, mainly because of the influence of a policy-driven accountability culture, motivated by No Child Left Behind, which holds educators responsible for learner outcomes. Although No Child Left Behind has been replaced by the Every Student Succeeds Act, the culture of accountability remains a driving force in education policy. Outcome-based accountability policies have greatly expanded the realm of work for school leaders. Prior to test score accountability, school leaders monitored teaching and learning so that the main stakeholders of the community—teachers, parents, community leaders, and sometimes students—would be satisfied with how things were working. Outcome-based accountability policies have pressed leaders to transform monitoring into a variety of data-driven practices that focus on school capacity to improve test scores for all students.

The biggest change with monitoring is the attention that educators must pay to integrating data on teaching and learning into daily instructional routines. Shifting the practices of monitoring from observation to data analysis draws a sharp line between the old and new practices of instructional leadership, while giving rise to a new set of organizational practices that we call *school information ecology*.[1] An information ecology approach to monitoring teaching and learning leads educators to think about everyday practices in terms of an instructional system through which information on practices can flow. From a school information ecology perspective, all kinds of information flow through professional practices and interactions. Learning information ecologies are organized to measure outcomes and also to provide feedback on the learning process. For students, this requires assessing what they produce; providing specific, critical feedback that can guide practice; and providing opportunities to try again. This same cycle is also necessary for professionals to learn new approaches to their work. Building information ecologies around multiple levels of student and educator learning is a key task for contemporary school leadership. CALL seeks to describe the practices that leaders use to design school information ecologies so that educators have the kinds of reliable and actionable information they need to improve teaching and learning practices.

The topics of CALL Domain 2 describe the practices schools need to gather information about the process and outcomes of teaching and learning:

SUBDOMAIN	CORE PRACTICES
2.1 Formative evaluation of student learning	Schoolwide practices provide feedback that students can use to refine their learning. These practices are built into the everyday practices of teaching.
2.2 Summative evaluation of student learning	The school collects information on the outcomes of learning, participation, and engagement that align with state standards and policies.
2.3 Formative evaluation of teaching	School leaders create pervasive opportunities for teachers to receive regular, ongoing feedback, coaching, and support in order to refine and improve teaching practices.
2.4 Summative evaluation of teaching	The school has developed reliable measures of the quality of teaching that integrate student outcome data.

The press to create schools that can produce higher test scores is a feature of the 21st-century policy context in many public schools.[2] We propose to situate the new data-driven monitoring practices in a narrative that traces the evolution from a prevalent, earlier model of organization that shaped 20th-century instructional leadership. The 20th-century standard, a loosely coupled system model, developed separate data systems in schools—one for teachers and another for leaders—that circulated different kinds of information relevant for the goals of each kind of actor. With the advent of accountability policies, school leaders needed to coordinate these separate systems in order to improve system outputs.

In this chapter, we begin our discussion of the practices in CALL Domain 2 by considering how accountability policies press leaders to tighten the relationship between teaching and leadership practices. We then consider how each of the components of Domain 2—summative and formative assessments for teaching and learning—can be enacted to create information ecologies in each school.

A BRIEF HISTORY OF ACCOUNTABILITY AND SCHOOLS: EMERGENCE OF A NEW MODEL OF INSTRUCTIONAL LEADERSHIP

The No Child Left Behind Act of 2002 (NCLB) transformed American schools. This landmark piece of legislation that reframed the question of what makes a quality school called for new standards for teacher certification and required schools to provide tutoring for students who struggled. It also mandated a system of test-based accountability for all public schools in the nation. All students at grades 3, 8, and 11 were required to take state-determined tests, and the data from the tests would be used to assess the quality of the school. Schools that did not meet test score targets were provided with additional support at the cost of school and district-level autonomy. Each state was required to create a website to communicate disaggregated test score and demographic information about every public school. Since NCLB, every teacher, parent, and community member (including realtors!) has access to performance and demographic information previously available only to school leaders and policymakers.

There has been much debate over the past decade about the effects of NCLB. But there is no denying that test score–based accountability has had a profound impact on the work of school leaders. Redesigning schools to meet the demands of test-driven accountability policies draws a sharp line between 20th- and 21st-century models of school leadership. Before NCLB, school leadership was often described in terms of loosely coupled systems. In organizational theory, the idea of coupling refers to the ways in which different aspects of a system interact with one another.[3] Tightly coupled systems have control processes that administrators can use to direct the system. In loosely coupled systems, the control mechanisms between organizational functions are weaker, and system components often operate independent of one another.

Leadership differs considerably in loosely and tightly coupled systems. In a tightly coupled system, leaders directly control system components to produce well-defined system outputs. Loosely coupled systems typically have multiple valid system outputs. The lack of a common agreed-on output, as well as the autonomy between system components, means that leaders in loosely coupled systems must exercise indirect leadership through such practices as regular interaction with community members.

In schools, loose coupling was particularly evident in the relation of instructional and administrative practices. Karl Weick observed that school leaders lacked direct control of the core practices of teaching and learning.[4]

American schools prior to NCLB lacked certain features of tightly coupled systems: rules for determining what counted as system goals and inspection practices to determine whether these goals were being met. Teachers had autonomy to direct the instructional practices of their own classrooms with limited guidance (or interference!) from school leaders. To shape the direction of the school, leaders relied on indirect methods that focused on strengthening the school's informal communication channels and social capital, such as building professional community, relational trust, or a shared vision of instruction to influence the practices of teaching and learning.

The lack of agreement on what counted as success in the school (and in the community) meant that different audiences assessed school quality in different ways. Parents might be impressed with the number of National Merit scholars prepared in the school; teachers were free to design and teach their own curricula; community members were satisfied with how many games the football team won. The lack of commonly recognized output measures meant that successful leaders sought to develop a shared understanding of school mission in the midst of diverse expectations. Instructional leadership was defined by mapping how school leaders prioritized teaching and learning in the tangle of competing demands.

NCLB changed the game by requiring schools to be held accountable for improving test scores for all students. It quickly became clear that the traditional practices of leaders in loosely coupled systems were no longer sufficient to spark test score improvement, mainly because leaders had little influence on what happened in the classroom. Improving outcomes for all students meant that leaders needed to get quality information about instructional processes. Leaders in the NCLB era need the ability to inspect and improve everyday classroom practices. This means creating stronger, shared practices of teacher observation, common assessments of classroom outcomes, and a shared curriculum that can guide the practice of teachers across classrooms. Teachers who cannot help students meet performance outcomes need to improve or be replaced. NCLB-inspired responsibility for outcomes has led to a tighter coupling between instruction and administration—between teachers and leaders. It also requires leaders to take more control over the instructional process.

Since NCLB, data have become the medium for instructional control. Test score accountability calls on the ability of schools to translate student outcome data into reformed instructional practices. Leaders began to draw on the skills of colleagues already trained in data analysis, including special educators and school psychologists, to make decisions about classroom instructional improvement.[5] Charter organizations have made headway in the education market with new models for how to organize data-driven instructional practice across schools. An emerging priority for education research has been to use methods from economics and program evaluation to identify what works for improving student test scores at scale.[6] A wave of private investment has resulted in an exploding market for data and communication tools, such as school information, benchmark assessment, and learning management systems.[7] Schools have become avid consumers of this new wave of data-driven management and are required to embrace a new brand of technocratic control that has transformed the loosely coupled leadership of the 20th century into the tightly coupled, information-intensive models of the 21st century.

This transition from 20th- to 21st-century school leadership has not been smooth. The cultures of autonomy in the loosely coupled organizations continue to struggle with the redefined roles of teachers, the breakdown of public employee unions, and the ways in which NCLB demands public sharing of internal data. Some scholars argue that the redefinition of teaching as the implementation of what works for all students has led to a widespread feeling of deprofessionalization among educators.[8] The relentless focus on test score outcomes has led some schools to game the system by focusing on test preparation activities at the expense of instructional time, narrowing the curriculum to focus on literacy and math (instead of science, social studies, and the arts) and outright centralized cheating.[9] Parents continue to resist the testing culture by opting their children out of testing.[10] The ongoing debate over the value of test-based reform continues as we consider common learning standards for all students, test-based teacher evaluation practices, and the development of national standardized tests.

Even as the debate about the value of standardized tests continues, the changes brought by NCLB are here to stay for school leaders—particularly in schools that address the needs of the students and families who struggle the most. Data-driven decision making has reshaped how we think about students with learning problems (response to intervention) and behavioral issues (positive behavior interventions and strategies). Nearly all schools now have school information systems, and most schools are using learning management systems to coordinate classroom work.[11]

Turning the clock back to the loosely coupled days of 20th-century leadership is not a viable option for 21st-century school leaders. This is not to say, though, that the best practices of 20th-century leadership have lost their value. We need the loosely coupled systems practices that respect teacher autonomy and the ability to adjust school capacity to emerging challenges now more than ever before. The worst trends of the 21st-century school reform are expressed in a technocratic culture of antipathy toward educators, in which teachers and leaders are seen as obstacles that slow progress toward achievement for all students. Reforms that aim to produce effects through the "fidelity of implementation" of programs shown to "work" across contexts (even despite contexts!) give rise to the illusion that school reform is a matter of technical management instead of a human process of teaching and learning.

Twentieth-century leaders in loosely coupled systems developed sophisticated indirect practices that in the best cases established resilient communities of professional expertise and autonomy that could adapt to changing student and community needs. Twenty-first-century accountability-driven leadership need not lead to deprofessionalizing practices for teachers and dehumanizing practices for students. The best contemporary school leaders bring together 20th-century skills of cultural development and professional community with the data-driven practices of 21st-century leadership:

- *Twentieth-century practices:* Building professional community; teacher autonomy and professionalism; developing a strong school mission around learning
- *Twenty-first-century practices:* Data-driven decision making; test score accountability; building assessment and feedback systems into everyday work of teaching, learning, and leadership

The CALL account of leadership practices to improve teaching and learning draws from the best ideas of each era. In this chapter, we describe the key practices developed in 21st-century school leadership to create an information ecology around the different kinds of information needed to guide teaching and learning. In Chapter 5, we turn to the best of 20th-century leadership as we describe the best practices in building professional community and relational trust through collaborative design. Once leaders focus the school community on improving learning, the CALL framework outlines how using data effectively and developing teacher capacity are the main pieces of a powerful engine of school improvement.

BUILDING INFORMATION ECOLOGIES TO SUPPORT TEACHING AND LEARNING

Monitoring teaching and learning describes how educators can observe and reflect on the processes and results of the core practices of the school: teaching and learning. In a world defined by information technologies, much of the work of monitoring takes place in the context of the generation, storage, and reflection on performance data.

We know that the kinds of information needed to assess the outputs of a system differ from what is needed to support learning. As we have noted, our discussion rests on a central distinction between summative and formative uses of data. Monitoring performance is organized around summative and formative data. Summative assessment reports on the results of a process, and formative assessment informs the process as it unfolds. In a typical classroom, grades are a common form of summative assessment. They are given at the end of a learning activity and rate students' work in terms of a standard of performance. Coaching is a type of formative assessment. Coaches provide feedback in the midst of a process so that learners can adjust their performance. Information ecologies have high-quality practices that provide summative evidence of the results of valued organizational processes, as well as formative feedback cycles that guide processes along the way.[12]

CALL describes the design of accountability-driven information ecologies in terms of a two-by-two table: formative assessments of learning and teaching and summative assessments of learning and teaching. Each set of practices generates and uses unique types of information; each set has a different audience for the information it produces. Together, these practices constitute the core elements of a school information ecology. It is the work of school leaders to ensure the adequacy of practices in each domain and to coordinate information flow across these organizational needs.

2.1 FORMATIVE EVALUATION OF STUDENT LEARNING

- Can students describe the goals of their learning?
- How do teachers collect and share information with students on their learning?
- Does the school have a system to collect and use formative information to guide student learning?
- Are school formative assessments aligned with performance on the state standardized test?

Formative assessment provides timely feedback in the midst of a process so that actors can adjust practices on the fly toward intended goals. Paul Black and Dylan Wiliam's (1998) work highlights the critical role that formative feedback plays in teacher-student interaction.[13] Learners need formative assessment to take control of their learning processes; teachers need formative assessment to connect instructional practices with student behaviors.

Formative assessment is an ongoing process that provides students and teachers with feedback on progress toward instructional goals. Schools that improve learning establish schoolwide practices for formative assessment of and by students, and teachers incorporate these kinds of assessment into their daily teaching practices. Instructional units are designed with formative measures of student knowledge at the start of the unit to inform its design and throughout the unit so that instruction can be geared toward ensuring that all students learn to high standards. Just as formative assessment guides instructional practice in the classroom, school improvement plans use course assessment data (such as student grade distributions, failure rates, attendance, and behavior) as formative data to guide the development of schoolwide improvement goals.

Providing formative feedback to learners in the midst of the learning process has proven to be among the most effective instructional strategies.[14] Teachers can assess the degree to which students are on task, comment and critique students as learning progresses, and invite students to engage in peer observation and critique each other's learning. Asking students to relate their learning processes to learning goals is a good indicator of the prevalence of student formative feedback.

One key indicator of the prevalence of formative feedback practices in the classroom is students' ability to explain what they are learning. At a basic level, CALL asked educators whether students could relate classroom activities to larger learning goals. Forty-six percent of educators stated that students could make this connection when asked, but 41% of the educators reported that they didn't know if students could make this connection. To get an estimate of the effects of these types of formative feedback practices, CALL invited educators to rate students' ability to explain their learning process. When asked about these kinds of "checks for understanding," 55% of CALL educators responded that they engaged in such practices at least once a week, and 12% responded that they didn't know how often these practices took place.

The most effective formative feedback strategies invite learners to generate information to monitor their own learning process in environments that support reflection, revision, and repetition. John Dunlosky and his colleagues identified several key component strategies, including reviewing lesson materials, highlighting and summarizing text, and building mental or physical representations of what the lesson means.[15] Presenting a representation of understanding could mean building a physical or virtual model, ranging from a mathematical model of a complex idea, to a film about issues in the local community, to a verbal account of the learning process in which students are engaged. Student-created representations allow students to provide a concrete example of their understanding that encourages them to fill in the gaps of what they know as well as an opportunity to provide feedback on what they know. While these types of activities could serve as summative assessments of student understanding, educators can read the characteristics of student representations as a complex indicator of where understanding is falling short and what kinds of activities to recommend for student improvement.[16] When students engage in these kinds of practices throughout their classroom experience, they take ownership of their learning and grow more comfortable with publicly displaying their own understanding.

From the perspective of systemic reform of teaching and learning in schools, teachers are also learners who need formative information to guide their practices. Students provide much of the information necessary for teachers to reflect on and adjust their own practices. Ninety-seven percent of the educators in the CALL survey reported collecting information on student learning to improve instructional practices. CALL asked educators to reflect on the kinds of information educators collect to inform their own instructional practices (Table 4.1).

These findings remind us about several features of how educators monitor student learning. First, 84% of educators recognize formative assessment as an important feature of setting and evaluating learning goals for students. The widespread use of formative assessment for students is a valuable foundation for building organizational capacity to improve learning for all students. The CALL survey did

Table 4.1 Frequency of Educators Using Formative Feedback Practices

TYPES OF INFORMATION	PERCENT OF EDUCATORS USING THIS KIND OF INFORMATION
Formative assessment	84%
Student grades	78
Student failure rates	71
Student attendance	66
Student discipline	66

not capture information about the quality of formative feedback practices; instead it asked about the presence and value of such practices. Still, it is not a far reach to claim that the familiarity and the frequency of formative feedback practices provide an excellent platform to refine the kinds of feedback that educators generate for and about students. Second, about three-quarters of educators use grades and failure rates, and two-thirds use attendance and discipline information to set and evaluate learning goals for students. These high numbers indicate pervasive data use in schools and demonstrate how monitoring student learning has already been transformed into a data-driven model.

A central addition to the formative feedback information ecologies in most schools is the benchmark assessment system.[17] This kind of feedback is formative for teachers in their ability to adjust instructional strategies to improve student outcomes. Products such as the Northwest Evaluation Association's Measures of Academic Progress (MAP) are computer-adaptive testing systems that provide reliable, immediate feedback on the progress students are making toward instructional goals. Benchmark systems provide a nationally normed profile for each student in a number of skill areas in math and literacy. MAP scores can then be used to determine the degree to which instructional practices are effective with students in terms of the school's learning goals.

Critics of benchmark assessment tools note that the information generated is typically not aligned with classroom curriculum, and instead of providing formative feedback on the learning process, it is used as a more frequent occasion for summative evaluation of learning outcomes.[18] This failure is not necessarily the fault of the benchmark system itself; it is a reflection of the degree to which school leaders have built processes to integrate benchmark data into the school information ecology. The challenge for leaders is to integrate the data generated by benchmark systems into the school improvement cycle. One challenge for this integration is to translate the benchmark data, which are aligned to learning standards, to lesson design, which is aligned to a particular instructional plan.[19] Another challenge is to create the time for educators to reflect on the benchmark data to make decisions about student placement and course redesign.[20] These kinds of practices point to the role that leaders play in designing organizational routines to make information actionable in classrooms.

Black and Wiliam often speak of formative feedback in terms of the ways in which teachers interact with students in classrooms.[21] Successful formative feedback is timely and situated in the learner's work, and it provides clear direction for successful revision. From a classroom perspective, this type of teacher-student interaction provides a model for successful learning. From a school leadership perspective, however, formative feedback sits at the heart of a layered information system for students, teachers, staff, and leaders. If we think of each level of people in the school as learners, then it is clear that each kind of actor needs information that is timely, situated in local practices, and provides viable options for revised action. System change adds two more aspects to formative feedback: it is linked to the work of other actors in the system and aligned with system goals.

2.2 SUMMATIVE EVALUATION OF STUDENT LEARNING

- How is student learning measured in the school?
- How are summative data used to set and evaluate progress toward meeting goals for improving outcomes?
- Do teachers and leaders examine the relation between student grades and student test performance?

Building the capacity to generate accurate outcome information on student learning has been one of the transformative challenges for school leadership today. Leaders and policymakers began to create this capacity by mandating standardized testing, pressing schools to engage in program alignment and encouraging test preparation for students.[22] Over the past decade, educators have refined the tools and practices that generate better summative information on the quality of teaching and learning in schools. For example, in the early stages of NCLB, standardized test producers were criticized for taking too long to get data back to educators and for not aligning test score results with the school curriculum. In response, schools moved toward more sophisticated forms of adaptive assessments that link student growth to specific curricular interventions and learning outcomes, and researchers began to develop tests that measure the "value added" by teachers to student learning in a new generation of achievement measures.[23]

These advances are not meant to demonstrate that contemporary schools live in a summative data utopia where all educators can measure what is valuable in learning. The challenge of linking summative information to the curriculum, the classroom, the teacher, and the student is still an ongoing program of research and development, and educators are consistently pressed into situations of using imperfect information to make high-stakes decisions about instructional quality. Many educators and researchers continue to question whether this ideal will ever be attainable. Yet as we have seen over the past decade, the drive toward better accountability-driven practices continues to press schools, educators, researchers, and assessment companies to advance the boundaries of measuring what students and teachers know and can do.

In the early stages of survey development, CALL explored whether schools were using summative data on learning in their schools. We found that the vast majority of schools used state test data and either owned or were using student information systems to manage assessment information.[24] Only one in five educators on the CALL survey reported not using state or district test scores for improving teaching and learning. Because of the frequency of the use of summative assessment tools, we moved on to explore the range of practices developed around turning summative testing data into information useful for improving teaching and learning. In addition to standardized tests, we discuss the prevalence and value of grading and test preparation as local tasks related to summative assessment.

Grading

At the local level, student grading practices provide summative indicators of student progress for most educators. Most of the educators in the CALL survey report that their schools have embraced standards-based approaches to grading. Only 20% of educators report that a standards-based grading program has not been developed in their school, and nearly two-thirds (62%) report that a standards-based system is being widely used in their schools. Almost 26% of elementary school educators report that standards-based grading helps to improve student learning (compared to 19% of high school educators).

When asked about the alignment of grade assignments to the state test, 60% of educators reported that most of the students with high grades are also proficient on the summative measure used for policy accountability. Interestingly, high school leaders were less confident about the relation between grading and testing. Thirty-four percent of administrators (compared with 21% of high school teachers) claimed that many students with high grades are not proficient on the state tests.

The validity of the relation between grading and testing is an ongoing challenge for educators to create systems that accurately measure student progress toward learning goals.[25] The alignment of summative measures of learning currently used in schools—grades, test scores, and progress reports—helps educators to develop a clearer signal about the quality of student learning outcomes.

Test Preparation

Seventy-five percent of educators surveyed reported that their students were involved in some form of test preparation activities. Thirty-five percent reported that such activities were regularly integrated into classroom teaching activities. Just 3 in 10 educators thought that the test preparation activities improved student understanding of the underlying content on tests. The main action on improving student learning, it seems, is located elsewhere in the instructional practices of the schools.

2.3   FORMATIVE EVALUATION OF TEACHING

- How often do teachers receive formative feedback?
- Do school leaders or colleagues regularly schedule time to talk with teachers about classroom practices?
- What types of support do teachers receive to improve their learning?

Formative data on teaching help to inform and improve instructional practices. Just as the ability to improve instruction does not magically emerge from test scores, the ability to systemically improve teaching does not flow naturally from rating teachers. Teachers and leaders need the same kinds of feedback to understand and refine their work. They need practice-level examples of how they ask and answer questions, information regarding whether students are thinking in the classroom, and how to respond to student work.

Good leaders create opportunities that allow teachers to reflect on formative feedback generated by peers and students. For many teachers, the ability to generate valuable formative feedback is simply part of being a professional. These teachers invite peers into their classrooms for feedback, regularly ask students about short-term and long-term learning, and reassemble lesson materials based on the feedback they receive. New teachers, or teachers who struggle to engage students, can learn to become professionals in a reflective context that invites feedback from multiple perspectives and builds formative feedback into the professional learning process. Schools that succeed in making teaching and learning practice public open up monitoring of professional practice so that the day-to-day work of the school becomes a data source for improvement.

Formative assessment for teachers and coaching and mentoring proved to be the two lowest-rated subdomains in the CALL survey. Schools across the sample, particularly high schools, reported infrequent opportunities to receive formative feedback and did not report much value in the largely generic, positive statements they received. When seen in the contrast between 20th- and 21st-century leadership priorities, the lack of quality formative feedback can be understood as a developmental process. Twentieth-century loosely coupled leadership left teachers on their own to refine teaching practices. Evaluation was often infrequent and resulted in information-poor feedback for most educators.[26] Twenty-first-century accountability-driven leadership prioritized higher-quality summative reporting on the quality of teaching but neglected to specify how to provide the kinds of formative feedback that would help to translate the results of testing into guidelines for improving teaching and learning. From an information ecology perspective, educators are learners who need specific, critical feedback on their efforts to improve. Significant effort has been invested in recent years in developing state policies that promote more frequent, systematic evaluation of teachers. The ability of these systems to promote more regular evaluation of teachers and provide helpful and formative feedback for all educators remains uncertain.

Formative feedback on teaching needs to be provided at several levels. First, teachers need eyes on their day-to-day work in classes. Postobservation conferences, for example, can provide formative feedback to educators. Nearly 70% of CALL educators reported that the formative feedback provided by observers and evaluators was helpful for improving their practice. The power of formative feedback comes when information is integrated into ongoing professional interaction. Thirty percent of educators reported that observers routinely followed up to see whether recommendations were helpful.

One problem in providing high-quality formative feedback to teachers may be the observers' content matter expertise. Educators in formal leadership positions may not have sufficient expertise in disciplinary content areas necessary to provide valued feedback. Pam Grossman, Alan Schoenfeld, and Carol Lee note that teachers need to know their subject matter and also the pedagogical knowledge necessary to successfully convey content to learners.[27] The nature of subject and pedagogical knowledge changes based on the discipline. Math teachers, for example, need to know math but also how to explain concepts in terms students will understand. They also need to recognize the typical mistakes learners make and know how to provide feedback for students to learn from their mistakes. In literacy learning, teachers need to know the processes of teaching reading and how to support students in communicating ideas through speech and writing. Understanding the content, how to teach it, and the ways that students come to learn the content are core competencies of successful teaching.

Giving high-quality formative feedback to teachers requires observers to be able to support each of these three core competencies. The ability to share feedback on each aspect of teaching, though, puts leaders in the difficult position of knowing the subject matter, teaching practices, and patterns of student understanding for each discipline. Barbara Scott Nelson and Annette Sassi describe this kind of expertise in terms of leadership content knowledge.[28] This form of knowledge guides what leaders notice during observations of teaching and the feedback they share with teachers about practice. Nelson and Sassi argue that it is impractical to require leaders to have all the subject matter and pedagogical knowledge teachers have. However, since most leaders were teachers at one time, the knowledge and skill of how subject matter informs pedagogy, which informs the ability to read student understanding, provides a powerful anchor for formative feedback.

Using their own experience as teachers and, more important, learners can help inform the quality of feedback for teachers. If leaders can take the stance as a learner in the classroom, they can observe how the lesson unfolds to students. This stance requires leaders to refrain from judgment about the quality of the lesson in order to notice questions raised by teacher and student interactions. Leadership content knowledge involves taking a stance as a learner and sharing observations about how the lesson is communicated from the perspective of the student.

In addition to feedback on classroom observations by school leaders, most schools integrate other kinds of formative feedback into their information ecologies. For example, 18% of CALL educators felt that peer observations were valuable practices, and 19% felt that peer coaching provided valuable feedback. In recent years, these kinds of practices have been repackaged and focused around specific instructional goals. Here we highlight three examples of some of these schoolwide programs for generating formative feedback on teaching: instructional coaching, walk-throughs, and instructional rounds.

Instructional Coaching

Instructional coaching has become a popular intervention as schools seek to provide personalized help for teachers to improve their practices.[29] Instructional coaching positions are typically designed to build the capacity of a school by providing teachers with formative feedback, as well as models of effective practices and conversations about student work and learning data.[30] Coaching is frequently introduced into schools as a part of a larger instructional intervention. For example, the My Teaching Partner program is designed to improve the quality of teacher-student interactions by helping teachers use the results of the Classroom Assessment Scoring System (CLASS).[31] My Teaching Partner uses videos of teaching practices to provide feedback for teachers. Coaches and teachers work together to build an action plan for teacher practice that results in new videos and further rounds of analysis. Coaching practices like My Teaching Partner help to focus improvement efforts around specific outcomes.

In practice, though, the work of instructional coaches is often unfocused and poorly defined. Melinda Mangin found that schools implemented coaching by adding a full- or part-time position dedicated to a variety of literacy support tasks with teachers or by simply adding responsibilities to an existing classroom teaching position.[32] Coaches are often required to do other kinds of work, such as supervision, substitution, and clerical work, or coaching is folded into more general job responsibilities like professional development or instructional resource coach. Even when it works, coaching is limited to providing customized help for small groups of struggling teachers.[33] The challenge for school leaders in providing effective instructional coaching appears to be resisting the temptation to use coaching time for other responsibilities and keeping the focus on formative feedback and continuous improvement for teachers.

Walk-Throughs

Walk-throughs are short, targeted visits to multiple classrooms for observers, typically school leaders, to get a better sense of what is going on in the school.[34] They are an important practice to help make formal leaders visible to teachers and students in the instructional process. Typically, walk-throughs focus on some aspect of the instructional process and allow observers to notice the degree to which the intended practice is visible in classrooms.[35] Observers decide ahead of time which specific practices they will note. These practices could range from the visibility of lesson objectives to patterns of behavioral interaction to the kinds of questions that students and teachers ask one another. Ideally, walk-throughs are followed by reflective conversations among the observers and then with the observed. In practice, though, educators may not use walk-throughs to make a connection to ongoing conversations about school improvement.[36] Making walk-throughs a routine practice for leaders in the school is an important step toward building a culture that makes teaching and learning practices public.[37]

Instructional Rounds

Instructional rounds are a specialized form of walk-through focused on providing feedback and building a culture of inquiry around a particular improvement goal.[38] They start with a shared problem of practice, such as improving math instruction, student engagement, or the use of instructional media in the classroom. Visits are organized to note how these goals are being addressed. Grounding observation in a shared problem allows educators to collect feedback on new approaches to instruction and design the next stage of work.

A central feature of the instructional round process is to train the community on what Elizabeth City and her colleagues call the "ladder of inference." This process guides observers to focus on what students are actually doing in classrooms (as opposed to what the teacher is doing or what students are supposed to be doing) as preparation for the community to reflect on the evidence they see (before then speculating on the causes for the evidence). A continuing focus on observation before conclusion trains the staff to consider "description before analysis; analysis before prediction; and prediction before conclusion."[39]

The shared focus of instructional rounds is both a strength and weakness in practice. A narrow focus on questioning in math or student explanation in literacy may provide help to teachers in those areas but would leave out the rest of the faculty. School leaders pressed to make resources stretch across the staff in order to provide some support for everyone may blur the aim of instructional rounds and diffuse the kinds of feedback that teachers would receive on the core instructional initiatives. Leaders who can keep the focus on a certain topic for instructional rounds can establish a discourse around these practices in the school, but then must find ways to attend to the needs of educators who do not teach in these domains.

2.4   SUMMATIVE EVALUATION OF TEACHING

- How often do leaders conduct classroom visits of each educator?
- Does the school use summative information to set and evaluate progress toward meeting school goals?

- Do formal teacher evaluation practices improve teaching?
- Are student test scores included in formal evaluations of teachers and staff?

Teacher evaluation in schools has had a rocky history. Prior to the NCLB accountability revolution, formal teacher evaluation was considered a necessary but ineffective practice to determine the quality of teaching. Evaluation practices were criticized for providing unreliable information, and practices often devolved into infrequent observations guided by checklists. The ratings that resulted from the application of evaluation frameworks resulted in most teachers receiving high ratings with little substantive information that could be used to understand the impact of teaching practices on student outcomes. In part, the unreliable information that resulted from contemporary evaluation practices meant that leaders could not gain insight into the quality of teaching practice.[40]

Teacher observation has been criticized as an unreliable method to gauge teacher quality, but it is still the predominant tool educators use to evaluate teachers.[41] Ninety percent of CALL educators reported that leaders observe probationary and nontenured teachers at least every semester—31% said that these kinds of observations happen every month for new and struggling teachers, and 75% said that all educators in their schools are observed annually. The data that result from observations are widely seen as valuable. Seventy-five percent of educators said that the observation data are used to set annual learning goals, and 67% said that the resulting conversations about observations helped educators to improve. Teacher observation continues to serve as a platform for schools to judge the quality of teaching.

The biggest change in post-NCLB evaluation practices is the inclusion of student test outcomes in teacher evaluation models. Using student outcome data to improve teacher evaluation systems will, according to advocates, result in better measurements of teaching quality.[42] Since the federal Race to the Top initiative in 2009, 30 states have moved to include some form of student test score outcomes in measuring educator effectiveness.[43] This rush to integrate student outcome measures into teacher evaluation has led policymakers, analysts, and educators to study and refine the relation between teacher and student performance.[44]

Some of the difficulties of connecting student test scores with teacher evaluation became clear early in the process. Simply linking the test scores of students to the time spent with teachers would not capture the effects of the teacher on learning. New value-added systems would need to measure what each teacher contributed to each student's learning. Teasing out the influence of individual teachers on individual students became a significant technical challenge that led to a flourishing new area of research in value-added measures to estimate what the teacher adds to the outcome scores of students.

Value-added measures have made important contributions to understanding the relationship between educational processes and outcomes. Erik Hanushek and Steven Rifkin found that replacing a teacher at the 25th percentile with a teacher at the 75th percentile of value-added performance would increase the learning gains of a typical student from the 50th to the 58th percentile of test score performance.[45] Eileen Horng and Susanna Loeb used value-added measures to show how strategic hiring and professional development practices define effectively building level leadership.[46] Raj Chetty, John Friedman, and Jonah Rockoff found that students assigned to high-value-added teachers were more likely to attend college, earn higher salaries after graduation, live in higher socioeconomic-status neighborhoods, and save more for retirement.[47] Research funders such as the U.S. Department of Education Institute of Educational Sciences and the Gates Foundation have made significant investments in refining value-added models to better capture the relation of teaching, learning, and outcomes in schools.

Still, value-added models have yet to realize their promise in measuring educator performance. Even as states embraced these new approaches as core pieces of their school improvement processes, critics have pointed out the dangers of making high-stakes judgments about teachers and schools based on value-added models. Linda Darling-Hammond and her colleagues summed up the problems with using value-added models for decisions about educators:

- *Ratings are not reliable.* Ratings for teachers and students vary from year to year even in the best value-added models.

- *Student skill and abilities matter.* Although the value-added models attempt to control for student backgrounds, teachers' ratings are affected by the ability and skill differences among students assigned to their classes.

- *Demographics matter.* Because students are not randomly assigned to classrooms, value-added models cannot eliminate alternative explanations, such as income, demographics, or life conditions, for why students might succeed or fail.[48]

The limitations of value-added measures as reliable indicators of teacher quality have led some states to abandon these models altogether and most states and districts to promote a multiple measure model that includes observations, test scores, and other forms of student and teacher data for summative evaluation of teachers.[49] The continuing debate about the adequacy of value-added assessment to capture the quality of teaching and learning will spur research to refine the accuracy of the analytical models and increase the capacity of researchers and educators to use sophisticated data tools in their efforts to create better models of teacher evaluation. The next-generation educator evaluation systems will likely include both improved measures of student learning and better observation frameworks to provide more accurate indicators of the quality of teaching in schools.

PUTTING IT ALL TOGETHER: INFORMATION ECOLOGIES FOR SCHOOLS

Building the capacity to respond to accountability policies has been one of the transformative challenges for instructional leadership today. Much of the pressure for making this change has led to transforming the resources and skills of loosely coupled systems into practices that accurately monitor and improve teaching and learning in a digital age. Leaders need to build information ecologies that provide accurate information on the quality and outcomes of instruction, as well as helpful information that can guide teachers and learners.

CALL's Domain 2 details the kinds of practices that educators and researchers from around the country identify as important for creating this new capacity for data-driven improvement. School leaders need to assemble information ecology components to inform the process of teaching and learning as well as the outcomes. Process measures alone make it difficult to direct improvement toward system goals; outcome measures alone do not create the capacity to adjust practices to meet system goals. At the student level, practices are needed to help students monitor their own learning process, provide clear paths for teachers to understand and provide accurate feedback to students about learning, and measure how students are making progress toward system achievement goals. At the teacher level, practices are needed to help teachers use examples of student work to reflect on their teaching, both give and receive feedback from peers on everyday teaching practices, and participate in evaluation systems that link teaching with student outcomes.

Successful leaders link together channels that collect and distribute both formative and summative assessment data in order to create information ecologies for learning. Summative data measure the system outputs and determine the goals toward which the school aims; formative data guide educators and learners in processes that realize system outcome goals. Information ecologies link formative data systems that measure learning processes with summative systems data that measure school outcomes.

Summative data to improve teaching and learning are created at two levels:

- *Summative evaluation of student learning:* The school conducts regular assessments of learning that align with state expectations and collects high-quality information on student participation and engagement.

- *Summative evaluation of teaching:* The school uses student outcome data to shape teacher evaluation routines that accurately capture the quality of teaching across the school.

The formative channels also have two components:

- *Formative assessment of learning:* Schoolwide practices provide feedback that students can use to refine their learning and are built into the everyday practices of teaching.

- *Formative assessment of teaching:* School leaders create pervasive opportunities for teachers to receive regular, ongoing feedback, coaching, and support in order to refine and improve teaching practices.

An information ecology is an evolving system of information practices aimed at creating an instructional system that improves learning for all students. The advent of data-driven approaches to monitoring teaching and learning is a distinctive feature of school leadership today. Policy leaders and education reformers have led the charge toward data-driven accountability by framing school success in terms of summative assessments of learning and teaching. The educators in the CALL survey report that they have widely implemented summative measures of teaching and learning in schools.

The CALL survey has found less evidence, however, of widespread implementation of the practices of formative feedback for students and teachers. Although the traditions of 20th-century leadership proved helpful in developing a shared sense of purpose in loosely coupled schools, this rich legacy of practices has not translated into the ability to use data to improve the learning process for teachers and students. Implementing high-stakes accountability policies is the first step in creating an information ecology that can meet the demands of accountability while also creating the capacity for improvement. Domain 3 of the CALL approach to school improvement builds on the 20th-century concept of professional communities of practice to describe how schools can develop the capacity to collectively learn from experience to improve practices. It defines the leadership work of designing professional community as a form of social capital that provides the capacity for schools to act on information to improve teaching and learning.

NOTES

1. Information ecology brings together Bonnie Nardi and Vicki O'Day's concept of an information ecology with Brigid Barron's idea of a learning ecology. An information ecology is a continuously evolving network of people, tools, and knowledge that characterizes practice in data-rich environments. Learning ecology adds the role that the learner plays in defining what counts as part of the information world. For more detail on their approaches, see Nardi, B. A., & O'Day, V. L. (1999); Barron, B. (2006).

2. This is particularly true of American schools. The 20th-century emphasis on local control of American schools and loose federal control has resulted in accountability cultures focused on meeting community expectations. Test score accountability, which has shaped the culture of most school systems around the world, has led American educators to listen to how their colleagues in other countries met the challenge of creating schools that intentionally improve test scores. For a rich discussion of the relations between the different types of accountability in schools across the world, see Leithwood, K. (2001).

3. The idea of loosely coupled systems dominated organizational perspectives on schooling during the 1980s and 1990s. Karl Weick's seminal 1976 paper, "Educational Organizations as Loosely Coupled Systems," defined the concept for thinking about schools. Richard Elmore's 2000 policy document, *Building a New Structure for School Leadership*, contrasted the practices of loosely coupled systems with the demands of standards-based accountability. Many of the main ideas from this section are drawn from the work of Weick and Elmore. See also Spillane, J. P., Parise, L. M., & Sherer, J. Z. (2011).

4. Weick, K. (1976).

5. Thomas, C. (2007); Halverson, R., & Thomas, C. (2007).

6. Slavin, R. E. (2002).

7. Burch, P. (2009).

8. For an overview of these trends, see Milner, H. R. (2013).

9. Nichols, S. L., & Berliner, D. C. (2005, March).

10. See, for example, Wallace, K. (2015, April 24).

11. Means, B., Padilla, C., & Gallagher, L. (2010).

12. The distinction between summative and formative data is not as rigid as it might appear. There is nothing inherent in the information itself that make data either formative or summative. The perspective of the user determines the difference between outcome and process data. For example, an aggregated student test score report can be a summative judgment to determine the success or failure of a school or of a particular educator, while at the same time it can be seen as feedback on a comprehensive reform initiative by a school or district leader. Furthermore, the features of the information suggest the ways in which the data are intended to be

used. A final grade in a class may well spark a student to change her learning process, but the typical letter grade lacks enough information to suggest what steps might be taken to improve. Good formative feedback information includes reference to the process that generated the data as well as guidance on how to proceed. Finally, in the accountability policy context, summative information is designed to trigger a learning process. Judging that a school, an educator, or a student is failing is supposed to be a first step toward beginning an improvement process. Thus, formative and summative information pathways need to complement one another in order to measure the outcome and the process of a system of teaching and learning.

13. Black & Wiliam (1998).
14. Black & Wiliam. (1998).
15. Dunlosky, J., Rawson, K. A., Marsh, E. J., Nathan, M. J., & Willingham, D. T. (2011).
16. Fred Newmann and his colleagues use the concept of authentic intellectual work to describe how educators can use student work to assess learning and provide formative feedback to both teachers and learners. See, for example, Newmann, F. M. (1996).
17. Christman, J., Neild, R., Bulkley, K., Blanc, S., Liu, R., Mitchell, C., & Travers, E. (2009).
18. See, for example, Shepard, L. (2010).
19. Prichett, R. (2007).
20. Halverson, R., Prichett, R. & Watson, J. G. (2007).
21. Black & Wiliam (1998).
22. Halverson et al. (2007).
23. Herman, J. L., Osmundson, E., & Dietel, R. (2010).
24. Our findings confirmed the work of Barbara Means and her colleagues that nearly all public K–12 schools used information systems to manage testing and accountability data. See Means, B., Padilla, C., & Gallagher, L. (2010).
25. See, for example, Bowers, A. (2011); Allensworth, E., & Easton, J. Q. (2007).
26. For more detail, see the discussion of CALL Domain 2.4 in this chapter.
27. Grossman, P., Schoenfeld, A., & Lee, C. (2007).
28. Nelson, B. S., & Sassi, A. (2005).
29. Gallucci, C., Van Lare, M. D., Yoon, I. H., & Boatright, B. (2010).
30. Mangin, M. M. (2014).
31. Pianta, R. C., Mashburn, A. J., Downer, J. T., Hamre, B. K., & Justice, L. (2008).
32. Mangin. (2014).
33. Mangin, M. M., & Dunsmore, K. (2015).
34. Protheroe, N. (2009).
35. Downey, C. J., Steffy, B. E., English, F. W., Frase, L. E., & Poston, W. K. (2004).
36. Grissom, J. A., Loeb, S., & Master, B. (2013).
37. Ginsberg, M. B., & Murphy, D. (2002).
38. City, E. A., Elmore, R. F., Fiarman, S. E., & Teitel, L. (2009).
39. City et al. (2009, p. 87).
40. For a discussion of the critiques of pre-NCLB evaluation practices, see Darling-Hammond, L., Wise, A. E., & Pease, S. R. (1983); Peterson, K. D. (1995); Loup, K. S., Garland, J. S., Ellett, C. D., & Rugutt, J. K. (1996); Halverson, R., Kelley, C., & Kimball, S. (2004).
41. Interestingly, the Gates Foundation's Measures of Effective Teaching project found that when teacher observations are guided by a research-based rubric, such as Charlotte Danielson's (2011) *Framework for Teaching,* they can yield modest but statistically significant predictors of student outcomes on standardized tests. The predictions are more accurate when made by

trained observers under experimental conditions, to be sure, but the study reminds us that we should not dismiss the power of the most widely used practices without analysis. See Kane, T. J., McCaffrey, D. F., Miller, T., & Staiger, D. O. (2013).

42. Glazerman, S., Goldhaber, D., Loeb, S., Raudenbush, S., Staiger, D. O., Whitehurst, G. J., & Croft, M. (2011); Odden, A. (2011).
43. Thirty-four percent of the CALL educators reported that student test scores were a substantial part of their teacher evaluation ratings. (Only 6% said that test scores were a primary focus of the ratings.)
44. National Council on Teacher Quality. (2013); Kane et al. (2013).
45. Hanushek, E. A., & Rivkin, S. G. (2010).
46. Horng, E., & Loeb, S. (2010).
47. Chetty, R., Friedman, J. N., & Rockoff, J. E. (2012, January).
48. Darling-Hammond, L., Amrein-Beardsley, A., Haertel, E. H., & Rothstein, J. (2011).
49. Cantrell, S., & Kane, T. J. (2013).

Domain 3: Building Professional Community

DOMAIN 3: BUILDING PROFESSIONAL COMMUNITY		TOTAL	ELEMENTARY	SECONDARY	LEADERS
		3.2	**3.2**	**3.2**	**3.2**
3.1	Collaborative schoolwide focus on problems of teaching and learning	3.5	3.5	3.4	3.7
3.2	Professional learning	3.5	3.5	3.5	3.6
3.3	Socially distributed leadership	3.2	3.2	3.1	3.4
3.4	Coaching and mentoring	2.6	2.7	2.6	3.0

Note: Five-point scale. $N = 18,677$ respondents.

RELATIONSHIPS ARE THE LIFEBLOOD OF ACTIVITY IN A SCHOOL community.[1] In their groundbreaking work, *Organizing Schools for Improvement: Lessons from Chicago*, Anthony Bryk and his colleagues at the Consortium on Chicago School Research summarized their decades-long research program that highlighted the role of trust and relationships as the key features of successful urban schools. They describe intricate networks of relationships among educators, learners, and families in need of constant tending.

Bryk and his colleagues describe the measure of the overall quality of interactions across the school community as *relational trust*.[2] Relational trust reflects the capacity of actors in an organization to ask for and receive help. At the organizational level, relational trust is a measure of the respect that colleagues have for one another to be respected and to take risks. When relational trust is present, people feel respected for their contributions even when others disagree; they feel the regard of others, trust that confidences are kept, and can rightfully expect that people will give their best effort to do what they say they will do. Relational trust functions as an organizational resource for school improvement. It reflects the capacity of the school community members to buy in to new projects and initiatives in the school and supports the diffusion of new practices among educators in the school.

Relational trust is best considered an outcome of a design that encourages certain kinds of professional interaction. It is a resource that can be developed through interactions in which professionals develop reputations for addressing the problems that community members bring forward. Over time, relational trust defines the school culture. If professionals persistently fail to solve problems of the community, the school develops a dysfunctional culture—and if the community develops pathways to successfully meet their challenges, the culture flourishes.[3]

The growth of relational trust does not happen accidentally. Leaders must create opportunities for educators, students, and community members to express problems to be solved. Each member of the community acquires a reputation for the ability to successfully address emergent challenges. We describe a certain kind of relational trust as *professional community*. Professional communities are designed to create the conditions for teachers to hear, share, and experiment with new ideas about practice.[4] When teachers take advantage of these opportunities to share their problems of instructional practice and when colleagues are able to help address these problems, a professional community around instruction begins to take root in the school.

Schools with strong professional communities have a clear sense of shared purpose and collective responsibility for student learning; professional inquiry among staff to achieve that purpose, including opportunities for sustained collaboration and reflection on practice; de-privatized teaching practices leading to norms of collegiality among teachers and leaders; and opportunities for staff to influence school activities and policies. Strong professional communities in schools that promote collective responsibility for student learning and norms of collegiality among teachers have been associated with higher levels of student achievement.[5] Professional communities describe the people resources that leaders can develop to improve practices of teaching and learning.[6] Leaders must create opportunities to develop relational trust that challenge, and ultimately replace, cultures that thwart collaboration. Lauren Resnick and Thomas K. Glennan speak of *nested learning communities* defined by the obligation of all community members to participate in the improvement efforts.[7] CALL Domain 3 draws on these advances to describe a set of tools that leaders can use to engage in activities that create relational trust through professional community.

The practices in CALL Domain 3 are arranged to support a theory of action for creating relational trust that results in professional community, which in turn comes to (re-)define school culture. Designing relational trust networks where teachers ask for and provide help about the emergent problems of instruction is the pathway toward building a resilient professional community around teaching and learning in schools.

Thinking about professional community in terms of relational trust recasts the efforts to build capacity in the school in terms of design. Leaders need to design new opportunities to spark interaction, structure design opportunities into new organizational routines, and build on these new routines to reinvigorate the school professional culture. CALL Domain 3 focuses specifically on how leaders and educators use the design of professional learning, socially distributed leadership networks, and coaching and mentoring to create professional communities that reshape the social fabric of the school into a resilient resource for change.

DESIGNING PROFESSIONAL COMMUNITY

CALL Domain 3 subdomains describe the richest, most pervasive opportunities to generate relational trust and professional community in schools. The model is described in four subdomains:

SUBDOMAIN	CORE PRACTICES
3.1 Collaborative schoolwide focus on problems of teaching and learning	Teachers regularly engage in collaborative school improvement planning, professional development, curriculum writing and mapping, and analysis of student work.
3.2 Professional learning	Professional learning is designed to achieve schoolwide goals and pinpoint teacher learning needs. It relies on external resources and local teacher expertise and creates networks for teachers to experiment and share best practices.
3.3 Socially distributed leadership	Decision making should cultivate teacher input on critical instructional and resource allocation decisions such as scheduling, budgeting, and extracurricular priorities.
3.4 Coaching and mentoring	Instructional coaches and mentors provide opportunities for expert teachers to build relationships that guide novice and struggling teachers to improve their practice.

The focus on problems of teaching and learning provides the goals and the motivations for developing professional community. Relational trust is developed through design activities that aim to solve the problems teachers face in their day-to-day work. Professional learning describes the heart of professional community in schools. Successful leaders orchestrate opportunities for educators to learn from one another, from students, and from community members as routine features of everyday interaction. Learning opportunities should happen throughout the school on different timescales—some aimed at immediate problem resolution and others at long-term changes to altering instructional routines. Socially distributed leadership shows how to support educators who emerge to take on greater responsibilities for leading. Coaching and mentoring support the work of new and struggling educators. Taken together, these subdomains describe the practices of strong professional communities that result in rich cultures of relational trust in schools.

3.1 COLLABORATIVE SCHOOLWIDE FOCUS ON PROBLEMS OF TEACHING AND LEARNING

- Do schoolwide meetings focus on design activities?
- How much do collaborative activities aim to improve teaching and student learning?
- Do teachers talk about the process and outcomes of student learning?

At the center of the Domain 3 is collaborative design focused on problems of teaching and learning. Schools have hundreds of problems to solve; leaders are responsible for identifying the problems worth solving and developing the pathways to design and implement solutions. Identifying which problems to address frames opportunities to create relational trust.

Faculty meetings and professional development provide the main tools leaders use to collaboratively design solutions to problems of teaching and learning. Eighty percent of CALL respondents reported that their school provided schoolwide professional learning opportunities. Leaders have precious little time to orchestrate interactions that can create relational trust among educators. Unfortunately, schoolwide meetings often did not provide a helpful resource for educators in CALL schools. Nearly 75% of educators in the CALL survey reported that the main focus of schoolwide meetings focused on announcements, school management issues, and presentations. School leaders and teachers disagreed about the uses of these times for interaction:

- Over 33% of leaders felt that schoolwide meetings provided opportunities for sustained interaction about teaching and learning, compared to only 20% of teachers.
- Eighty percent of teachers felt that schoolwide meetings provided little or no help for improving their practice compared to nearly 40% of leaders who claim the time is helpful.

Educators did not see the intentions of leaders to design opportunities for meaningful interaction as valuable. For many educators, faculty time failed to spark the kinds of interactions that lead to professional community.

However, there is another side to the story. When asked about the benefits of specific kinds of interactions, it becomes clear that educators in many schools value the quality of certain kinds of faculty interaction:

- Fifty-six percent of educators reported that professional development planning significantly improved their practices.
- Forty-six percent reported the same effects for curriculum writing.
- Forty-five percent reported positive effects from school improvement planning activities.
- Eighty-five percent of teachers reported that they interacted daily or weekly with colleagues with ideas about teaching and learning.

These kinds of activities, from professional development to curriculum writing and school improvement planning, describe more long-term opportunities for sustained interaction with colleagues. Interaction around these kinds of instructional tasks can spark reciprocal requests for help as educators work through the complexity of designing plans for themselves and for the school. In other words, when teachers seek out and receive advice from one another about core instructional tasks, the school develops relational trust.

Bryk and colleagues write of structuring opportunities that encourage teachers to willingly "take on extra work as they engage colleagues in planning, implementing and evaluating school improvement activities."[8] Regular interaction where the outcome of the process is both uncertain and dependent on the quality of interaction can facilitate "social exchanges among school professionals as they seek to learn from one another in the trial-and-error phase of implementing new practices."[9] When educators are presented with safe, creative spaces to develop new answers, they can begin to ask for the kinds of help and to provide the kinds of support that shape a robust network of relational trust in a school.

3.2 PROFESSIONAL LEARNING

- What forms of professional learning do teachers in the school use?
- How much of an impact does professional learning have on teaching practices?
- What kinds of evidence are used to assess the effectiveness of schoolwide professional development activities?

Professional learning is at the heart of a strong school culture. Researchers have shown that sustained professional learning is related to student achievement gains.[10] When people learn, they acknowledge what they do not know, seek support and resources for improvement, and experiment with what they have learned. Learning is a natural activity for cultivating relational trust, if only because people typically ask for help in the learning process. Educators learn in the same ways as everyone else. Most learning is sparked by individual interest—either a failure to perform at an expected level or a desire to expand horizons (or both). The outcomes for individual learning are unpredictable under the best conditions. Sometimes learners lose interest, sometimes they fail to see the process all the way through, and other times what they learn is not strong enough to change practices.

Organized professional learning in schools takes the process to another level. These types of activities are designed to include all educators (whether they are interested or not) in learning common knowledge and skills. Creating these schoolwide opportunities for learning is a core task for school leaders. Eighty percent of CALL educators reported that their schools developed and used a schoolwide professional learning program. Successful design for professional learning first requires cultivating the interests of community members, providing a safe space for exploring and experimenting with new ideas, providing feedback on the learning process and the results of new practices, and structuring opportunities to revisit and adjust the original ideas learned.

Schoolwide efforts to promote professional learning often fail in ways that disillusion community members. In part, the failure of the design of learning opportunities is rooted in the nature of professional practice in organizations. Chris Argyris's work suggests that knowledge professionals paradoxically are notoriously resistant to learning.[11] Consultants, lawyers, doctors, financiers, and, yes, teachers are typically hired for what they know and can do. Professional learning requires them to acknowledge, often publicly, that their expertise is lacking and that their skills are in need of improvement. Argyris found that the perceived risk of public embarrassment encouraged professionals to do anything to resist engaging in new learning. Professionals would critique clients, question the data, point out inconsistencies in interpretation, doubt the need for the new information, and undermine the providers of professional learning—anything to avoid the painful public examination of inadequacy that would accompany experimenting with new skills.

Argyris and his colleague Donald Schön developed the concept of single- and double-loop learning to design for successful professional learning.[12] Single-loop learning describes how most professional learning models are designed.

Single-loop learning activities provide training and then release learners to try out what they have learned in practice. These models are typically easy to design and implement, and they can be readily adapted to provide training on new topics. It is easy to bring in a speaker or organize a discussion around a new school safety policy or a new parent engagement program. The value of single-loop learning models is to efficiently introduce new information into a context. The disadvantage is that these models provide little guarantee of sparking changes in practice. The straightforward nature of single-loop learning typically overlooks and neglects to elicit the ideas, practices, and values already in play for learners, and there is no check to see whether learners could actually use the new ideas in practice.

Double-loop learning seeks to activate what Argyris and Schön call the learner's *theory-of-action*. The theory has two parts: the espoused theory, which is how a person explains his or her behavior, and the theory-in-use, which may not be articulated by or even accessible to the learner, guides the actual behavior. In a typical professional learning situation, the espoused theory of the actor is engaged, but the theory-in-use is left untouched. Argyris and Schön's double-loop learning is designed to bring the theory-in-use into conflict with the espoused theory by inviting learners to articulate what they expect to happen, then to provide critical and supportive feedback on the results of trying the new ideas out in public in order to guide new practice.

Successful double-loop learning creates a relational trust network. Bringing theories-in-use into the light of day through experimenting with new practices allows learners to adjust the principles that really motivate behavior and create more alignment between espoused and enacted theories. Argyris and Schön suggest that professional learning can take place when the theory-in-use is transformed through experimentation, feedback, and collaborative support. Double-loop learning creates relational trust to support learners in taking the risk to learn new practices.[13]

The design of professional learning opportunities should create relational trust by building new knowledge and skills among all educators and support staff in the school. Designing for double-loop learning requires leaders to build cycles of reflection, design, implementation, feedback, and practice into the everyday culture of being a professional. Leaders responsible for designing effective learning must attend closely to building safe spaces for new practices to take root.

3.3 SOCIALLY DISTRIBUTED LEADERSHIP

- How do school leaders encourage teachers and staff to share best practices with other staff members?
- How does the school invite participation in decision making?
- How are teachers and staff encouraged to support the work of others?

Socially distributed leadership describes how educators across the school participate in leadership tasks. Formal leaders, such as principals, department chairs, lead teachers, and student services coordinators, have official responsibility for making sure these tasks are done. Often, though, people who are not formal leaders, including teachers and staff, participate in leadership tasks. Teachers typically take on central responsibility for monitoring student learning (Domain 2), maintaining the norms of professional community (Domain 3), and establishing safe learning spaces in their classrooms (Domain 5).

The term *socially distributed leadership* is a call for formal leaders to empower teachers as leaders. Simply recognizing the leadership roles that teachers play can help to turn around an authoritarian discourse that diminishes the control teachers have in the workplace. Richard Ingersoll suggests that "schools need to go beyond holding teachers more accountable. They need to give teachers more control."[14] Kim Farris-Berg and her colleagues explain that the culture of the school changes when teachers are given the autonomy to take on leadership tasks.[15] They document eight ways that leadership changed when teachers were given more autonomy:

- School initiatives became focused on the needs of students as individuals.
- Collaboration was envisioned as schoolwide (versus classroom specific).
- Educators and students were encouraged to be active, ongoing learners.
- Instructional initiatives emphasized individualized learning.
- Disciplinary issues were seen as dependent on the quality of teaching.
- Measures of student achievement moved beyond test scores.
- Teacher evaluation focused on peer coaching and evaluation.
- Budgeting was based on meeting student needs.

Teacher leadership focuses schoolwide activities on addressing the needs of learners. Domain 3.3 encourages schools to both recognize the role that teachers play in engaging in leadership tasks and allow educators to shape the roles of leadership toward addressing the needs of learners.

Leaders can also reward and encourage teachers to pioneer innovation. The legend of maverick teachers—those who make a special effort to connect with students using innovative methods and challenging bureaucratic limits—lives on in movies and in schools. Catherine Cornbleth found that mavericks viewed the typical problems that classroom teachers face as challenges to be overcome.[16] According to Cornbleth, they get results by connecting with student experience, using humor and unconventional strategies in their teaching, and making personal connections with students as a pathway for risk taking in the classroom.

The problem with mavericks in many schools, though, is that they are isolated and encouraged to work alone. They are ignored and sidestepped in schoolwide improvement activities and end up being ostracized as outsiders. Savvy leaders recognize mavericks as innovative sources of organizational change. Leaders must develop relational trust networks that invite teachers to consult mavericks about new practices but also encourage mavericks to ask colleagues for help. This kind of reciprocal relationship will draw innovative practitioners into the school community and lower the cultural barriers that isolate mavericks. School leaders must allow mavericks to take on new roles so that the distribution of leadership can include, instead of segregate, zones of innovation within the school.

3.4   COACHING AND MENTORING

- Do school leaders encourage expert or experienced teachers to mentor their colleagues?
- How do instructional coaches spend their time with teachers?
- Are there effective induction and remediation programs for new and struggling teachers?

How do leaders support teachers who struggle with the routines and expectations of the school? New teachers can struggle with the transition from preparation to real-life schools; some experienced teachers commit to practices that have worked over the years in ways but now stunt their development of new skills and knowledge. Vibrant professional communities include opportunities for all members to develop relational trust, both offering and receiving help in learning. Coaching and mentoring are two research-proven strategies schools have used to distribute learning opportunities across the community.

Michael Fullan and Jim Knight describe how coaches work with teachers to plan and model lessons, observe instruction, facilitate meetings, and collaborate in grading and discussion data. "Next to the principal," they write, "instructional coaches are the most crucial change agents in schools."[17] Coaches play a central role in providing customized help for teachers to improve practice, provided mainly in conversations in which help is offered to and, in time, asked for by teachers. Coaching can thus become a key source of developing relational trust and promoting double-loop learning in schools. Coaches and teachers can engage in the kinds of one-to-one interactions that surface tacit theories-in-use and can help teachers to experiment and receive feedback on new strategies and receive feedback. Coaching is at the heart of the professional learning process for many teachers.

Mentoring programs gained popularity in the 1980s and 1990s as a strategy to support new and struggling teachers. Leslie Huling and Virginia Resta discuss how much of the early research on mentoring focused on the value to the mentees.[18] Pairing new teachers with mentors who work in the same subject area and collaborate regularly on lesson planning and observation has the best chance of improving teacher retention.[19] Later research showed that mentors reported improvements in the quality of their own teaching, learned to ask better questions, provided nonjudgmental feedback, and developed new ideas about teaching and assessment.[20] These reciprocal benefits demonstrate the value of mentoring as an important tool for induction, retention, and professional learning.

The benefits of coaching and mentoring depend on the quality of implementation. Research is mixed about the effects of coaching and mentoring as schoolwide strategies. Even when they are perceived as valuable to participants, studies have shown that practices frequently do not improve teaching. Worse, mentoring and coaching can reproduce the dysfunctional interactions of toxic school cultures.[21] Districts often implement coaching to target school- and district-wide learning priorities such as improving literacy teaching and outcomes for all teachers. These kinds of programs provide help that teachers do not ask for. In addition, coaches and mentors may fail to challenge the existing theories-in-use of learners, and the new practices may simply live alongside the old practices.[22] If coaching and mentoring are to become valuable tools for sparking relational trust, they must engage learners in double-loop learning.

PUTTING IT ALL TOGETHER: DESIGN AS A MODEL FOR BUILDING PROFESSIONAL COMMUNITY

What would a design model of professional community based on relational trust look like in a contemporary school setting? As we have discussed, double-loop learning is at the heart of what makes a design process work. In design, participants must articulate what they think is going to happen in what they build. When designers have to use what they make or, better, when they get a chance to watch others use what they make, they learn about how their theories-in-use are brought to light and challenged in actual practice. Learning from the feedback of seeing your ideas used in the world is a powerful incentive to alter your theory-in-use to create more effective solutions. When leaders orchestrate collaborative design activities into professional learning, coaching, and mentoring, educators can together develop a culture of risk taking where colleagues become resources for deeper learning. Relational trust develops when educators look to one another for help; professional community describes the culture that results from layered interactions of relational trust.

The following sections describe several examples that bring educators together in promising collaborative design activities that have been shown to result in robust professional communities: video clubs, lesson study, and networked improvement communities.

Video Clubs

Miriam Sherin and Beth van Es developed the video club model as a way for educators to observe and reflect on their own teaching.[23] Video clubs invite teachers to tape their own classroom practice and set up collaborative reflection sessions for teachers to discuss what they see. The purpose of the clubs is not to evaluate the quality of the teaching; rather, Sherin suggests, collaborative reflection helps teachers to develop professional vision, that is, the ability to "notice and interpret significant features of classroom interaction." This capacity to notice and interpret the features of each other's practice creates a strong sense of community as teachers begin to ask for and receive help in improving their own practices. Professional community that springs from activities like video clubs can quickly transition to discussions about shared issues with new practices underway in the school and discussions about which aspects of practice are promising areas for exploration.

Lesson Study

Lesson study began in Japan as a pathway for educators across the country to coordinate the design of a national course of study.[24] A group of grade-level teachers in a school chooses a particular lesson for their professional learning focus. Each teacher designs a version of the lesson; then the teachers observe one another teaching the designed lessons and note the characteristics of the implemented lesson. Teachers consider the example actions used to explain concepts, the question prompts that best drew out student interest, and the assessment activities that captured what and how students are learning. Teachers meet as a group throughout the process to converge on a single design, test the design in each other's classroom, and conclude by writing a curriculum to submit to the national lesson study network.

Lesson study includes all the key features of double-loop learning. Teachers express tacit theories-in-use about the effective strategies for instruction and build lessons based on their best guesses in design activities. They reflect on their own approach by observing one another's classrooms and coming to a shared understanding of a new approach that replaces their prior lesson. Lesson study requires teachers to ask for and receive help from one another about the design process. Leaders work with teachers to select lessons that are important to the local community and desirable to the national curriculum movement as well.

The presence of an authentic audience, both local and national, is another aspect of the feedback process that makes design authentic for teachers. Colleague networks around the country become known for the quality of their contributions to the national course of study, and it becomes a matter of local pride for educators to participate in national efforts to improve teaching and learning through lesson design.

Networked Improvement Communities

Networked improvement communities provide a promising model for iterative integration that Anthony Bryk and colleagues call "coordinating professional learning cycles."[25] These communities are organized around collective approaches to problem solving that are

- Focused on a well-specified common aim
- Guided by a deep understanding of the problem, the system that produces it, and a shared working theory to improve it

- Disciplined by the methods of improvement research to develop, test, and refine interventions
- Organized to accelerate their diffusion out into the field and effective integration into varied educational contexts

Like lesson study, networked improvement communities use problem setting and design to guide local educators toward addressing persistent problems of practice. Beyond lesson study, though, these communities work on problems in the classroom and across the organization. Community members stretch their expertise in a variety of problem-solving cycles that invite opportunities to ask for and receive help. Networked improvement community leaders work with members to select challenges that build on prior problem-solving activities and create channels to disseminate the solutions from prior work across national professional organizations. Together, Bryk and his colleagues suggest, these cyclical efforts to frame and solve persistent problems of practice become improvement science, a new model for professional learning in organizations.

LESSONS FOR BUILDING PROFESSIONAL COMMUNITY IN SCHOOLS

We have suggested that the foundation for school improvement is organizing professional learning around activities that create relational trust. When schools have strong relational trust, members ask for and receive help from one another, and the expertise in the community itself becomes a resource for improving practices of teaching and learning. Focusing on the problems of teaching and learning helps to create relational trust around the issues that matter in schools, and double-loop learning activities that involve design invite educators to reflect on and change their prevailing theories-in-use. A successful professional community integrates individual interest, design, organizational capacity, and data-driven measures of progress into a dynamic system of learning. In the hands of savvy leaders, tools such as discussion clubs, video clubs, lesson study, and networked improvement communities are valuable pieces for building professional community in schools.

The capacity of a school to learn and engage in new practices is best described as professional community. The culture of a school is shaped by its existing professional community. Interactions that create relational trust can result in strong professional communities in schools. Leaders need to engage educators in problems worth solving and orchestrate the resulting experiences into new opportunities for generating relational trust. Professional learning should consist of organizing design activities across the school to address emerging problems. When educators design together, they can reshape the culture of any school.

NOTES

1. Bryk, A. S., Sebring, P. B., Allensworth, E., Luppescu, S., & Easton, J. Q. (2010).
2. See also Bryk, A., & Schneider, B. (2002).
3. Kent Peterson and Terry Deal discuss a wide variety of strategies for educators to transform school culture. They draw on the Four Frames to suggest actions that alter the structures, politics, human resources, and symbolic interaction in organizations. We will argue that the CALL relational trust strategy of building relational trust around core practices gets to the heart of the school's culture and that the practices that Bolman and Deal suggest are well suited to maintain and extend the new culture brought about by changes in relational trust. See Bolman, L. G., & Deal, T. E. (2008).
4. For more information on the relation of professional communities to school change, see Louis, K. S., Kruse, S., & Bryk, A. S. (1995); Bryk, A., Camburn, E., & Louis, K. S. (1997); Newmann, F. M., & Wehlage, G. G. (1995); Youngs, P., & King, M. B. (2002); Supovitz, J. A., & Poglinco, S. M. (2001).
5. See, for example, Lee, V. E., & Smith, J. B. (1996); Little, J. W. (1982); Louis, K. S., Marks, H. M., & Kruse, S. (1996).
6. While many schools have developed a sense of community among the adults, not all communities can be described as professional. A professional community is more than a shared sense of collegiality. Having people get along in the school is not the same as having a robust, shared capacity for change among adults. Pam Grossman, Alan Schoenfeld, and Carol Lee (2007) traced how the development of professional community can go awry. Simply inviting faculty members to participate in a regular meeting of a book discussion club was not enough to spark professional community. In the case they studied, they found that faculty did not challenge each other's assumptions in the book club discussion and stayed safely within school culture of not challenging the opinions of colleagues. They concluded, "We have little sense of how teachers forge the bonds of community, struggle to maintain them, work through the inevitable conflicts of social relationships, and form structures for social relationships over time. Without such understanding, we have little to guide us as we create community" (p. 6). Grossman and her colleagues used this example to show how efforts to build professional community often result in pseudo-communities where the desired practices for interaction falter in the face of school culture. Simply putting professionals together in a common place for discussion about important topics is insufficient to create professional community. Schools must go beyond conversation to spark real change in school cultures.
7. Resnick, L. B., & Glennan, T. K. (2002).
8. Bryk, A. S., Sebring, P. B., Allensworth, E., Luppescu, S., & Easton, J. Q. (2010).
9. Bryk et al. (2010, p. 141).

10. For a review of this work, see Darling-Hammond, L., Wei, R. C., Andree, A., Richardson, N., & Orphanos, S. (2009).

11. Argyris, C., & Schön, D. A. (1974).

12. Argyris & Schön. (1974).

13. This focus on developing learning environments through opportunities to build on what learners already know is, of course, the guiding insight of constructivist theories of learning. For an overview, see, for example, Fosnot, C. (1996); Smith, J. P., diSessa, A. A., & Roschelle, J. (1993). From a cognitive perspective, research on conceptual change emphasizes how instruction that does not engage with underlying mental models typically results in two-level outcomes in which learners can successfully respond to test questions but cannot use new ideas to explain anything. Successful instruction requires teachers to construct situations that elicit tacit theories from students through a process of making hypotheses about possible action, then examining the results of hypothesis testing and practice new explanations that satisfy what learners see is happening in the learning environment. When this cycle of elicitation-hypothesis formulation-explanatory reintegration is repeated as a routine process of instruction, learners can begin to change underlying theories-in-action about the world through direct, public (and social) guidance. For more information on conceptual change in learning, see Carey, S. (1985); Chi, M.T.H., & Slotta, J. D. (1993); and DiSessa, A. A. (2001).

14. Ingersoll, R. (2007).

15. Farris-Berg, K., Dirkswager, E. J., & Junge, A. (2012).

16. Cornbleth, C. (2008).

17. Fullan, M., & Knight, J. (2011).

18. Huling, L., & Resta, V. (2001).

19. Ingersoll, R., & Kralik, J. M. (2004).

20. Clinard, L. M., & Ariav, T. (1998); Gordon, S., & Maxey, S. (2000).

21. For a review of the research on the effects of coaching and mentoring initiatives, see Darling-Hammond et al. (2009).

22. Mangin, M. M. (2014).

23. Sherin, M. G., & van Es, E. A. (2009); van Es, E. A., & Sherin, M. G. (2010).

24. Hurd, J., & Lewis, C. (2011).

25. Bryk, A. S., Gomez, L., Grunow, A., & LeMahieu, P. (2015).

CHAPTER SIX

Domain 4: Acquiring and Allocating Resources

Domain 4: Acquiring and Allocating Resources

DOMAIN 4: ACQUIRING AND ALLOCATING RESOURCES		TOTAL	ELEMENTARY	SECONDARY	LEADERS
		3.2	**2.8**	**2.9**	**3.3**
4.1	Personnel practices	3.3	2.9	2.9	3.5
4.2	Structuring and maintaining time	3.4	3.2	3.2	3.5
4.3	School resources focus on student learning	3.1	2.8	3.0	3.3
4.4	Integrating external expertise into the school instructional program	3.0	2.7	3.0	3.2
4.5	Coordinating and supervising relations with families and external communities	3.1	2.7	2.6	3.2

Note: Five-point scale. $N = 18,677$ respondents.

W E STARTED OFF THE BOOK WITH A DEFINITION THAT "SCHOOL LEADERS establish the conditions for improving teaching and learning." What exactly does this definition mean? What are the conditions, and how do leaders establish them? Much of the work of leadership is setting the stage so that others can succeed. When this work is done well, there is not much glory in being a school leader. The first thing you might note from the table at the start of this chapter is that administrators rate their schools higher in Domain 4 practices than teachers do. Much of the work we describe in this chapter—setting up time to meet, bringing external expertise into the school, building relationships with the community—can be invisible to those not directly affected. Most of the day-to-day work of leaders is responding when things break down and cleaning up the messes of other people. Some of the work, though, has a longer time frame and involves planning for interaction and setting up teachers and learners to succeed.

The conditions must be put in place for a thing to happen. Each CALL domain describes a different kind of condition for success. Domain 1 considered the story that leaders live and tell to define the mission of the school in terms of student learning. Domain 2 documented the information resources schools need to improve the processes and outcomes of learning. Domain 3 discussed how to improve the skills and experiences of educators through the design of professional community. Each of those domains focuses on how leaders work with educators. Education is a human enterprise, and effective management of human resources is a key determinant to school success. In most schools, fully 80% of the cost of education is allocated to the people who interact with students in the classroom.[1] Educators are the main resources through which leaders can work to improve learning. It is not surprising that so much of successful leadership work aims at establishing the conditions for educators to succeed in their work.

In the final two CALL domains, we share how leaders work with money, time, space, external expertise, and local communities to establish conditions for improving learning. These resources support teachers and learners by creating safe and effective environments for learning. Domain 4 describes how leaders acquire and allocate money, time, expertise, and community interaction to support effective teaching and learning. In Domain 5 we turn to the design of the learning environment itself to consider how leaders work with educators and students to build safe and inclusive spaces where all learners can thrive. Taken together, the CALL domains describe the range of work that researchers have shown and educators have created to establish the conditions for improving teaching and learning.

This chapter on the fourth CALL domain focuses on the management of human and financial resources. We examine distributed leadership practices related to the acquisition and allocation of money, people, time, and interaction. In our conversations with school-level leaders and educators, we encountered some resistance to the idea that local actors have control over money and people. Many school leaders work in districts that specify how much money each school gets, the time it can spend on discretionary interaction, and which teachers it can hire. Working in these kinds of schools gave educators the sense that they could work only with what was given, and this lack of control over resources considerably limited their ability to shape the environment. Straitjacketed by circumstance, these leaders saw their work as implementing what the district required—that is, doing what they were told.

Other leaders, though, in the very same circumstances, emphasized that there are always decisions to be made about how resources are acquired and allocated. Sometimes these decisions are subtle matters of emphasizing certain program goals. Sometimes local leaders build relationships with donors to support local initiatives. But, these leaders say, to resign their discretion to decisions made by others is to forfeit their ability to shape the learning environment. Our approach in Domain 4 is to ground the practice of most school-level leaders in a district context, but also to emphasize what most leaders can do within these contexts to accomplish the work that needs to be done. Every day, creative school leaders repurpose obstacles into valuable resources for learning. The practices of Domain 4 encourage leaders to take an active designer mentality toward their work by interpreting every kind of resource by its potential to enable best practice.

DOMAIN	CORE PRACTICES
4.1 Personnel practices	Personnel practices guide how new teachers are inducted and programs that reward teachers for high performance and effectively address poor performance.
4.2 Structuring and maintaining time	Teacher and student time is scheduled to maximize student learning opportunities.
4.3 School resources focus on student learning	School leaders acquire and allocate resources to help struggling students and improve student learning.
4.4 Integrating external expertise into the school instructional program	School leaders connect teachers to external resources in the district and academic communities to support student learning needs.

DOMAIN	CORE PRACTICES
4.5 Coordinating and supervising relations with families and external communities	The school takes an active role in building relationships with families and community groups. Meetings with parents are convenient, well attended, and facilitate effective communication.

4.1 PERSONNEL PRACTICES

- Is there a formal program in place to induct new teachers into the school?
- Are teachers rewarded for high-quality teaching performance?
- Are there meaningful consequences (support for improvement, reassignment, or termination) that are consistently applied to address chronically poor performance?

In Chapter 5 we discussed the power of bringing teachers together in design activities to create the capacity for improvement through professional community. Here we examine how schools develop personnel practices to support new teachers and teachers who struggle.

New Teacher Induction

New teachers are a precious resource for a school community. It is difficult to make the transition as a new employee into any organization, but schools are particularly challenging because teachers primarily work in isolation in their classrooms. Leaders need to design processes to acculturate new teachers into the norms of the school. It will not happen effectively without purposeful attention to creating induction supports to help new teachers understand how the school works and address inevitable problems that arise for those teaching in a classroom setting for the first time.

Teacher induction is important not just because there are so many first-year teachers (over 200,000 across the country each year), but because new teachers have very high turnover rates. Approximately 40% to 50% of teachers leave in their first five years. Research by Richard Ingersoll and his colleagues has found that the shortages of minority teachers and math and science teachers are not due to a lack of teacher supply but, rather, to high attrition by these groups early in their teaching careers. Moreover, he found that departing teachers report that a key reason for leaving is the lack of support that they received from their schools.[2]

Teacher induction programs ease the transition of new teachers into the classroom by organizing resources to address problems of practice early in their careers. Ingersoll and his colleagues examined what types of induction programs were offered and what their impact was on teacher retention:

> The most common package [for new teachers] consisted of just two basic components: working with a mentor and having regular supportive communication with one's principal, another administrator, or one's department chair. Beginners receiving just these two supports had better retention than those who received no induction at all, but the difference was small. In contrast, other beginners received a far more comprehensive package: the above two supports plus others, such as participation in a seminar for beginning teachers, common planning time with other teachers in the same subject, a reduced course load, and assistance from a classroom aide. Getting this comprehensive package had a very large effect; the likelihood that beginners who received this package would leave at the end of their first year was less than half that of those who participated in no induction activities.[3]

The CALL data examine the existence of induction programs for teachers and their effectiveness in improving student learning. Thirty-six percent of elementary teachers and 32% of secondary teachers report that their school did not provide teacher induction support (induction programs for new teachers do not exist, are being developed, or are developed but not used). Forty-five percent of teachers reported induction programs that are used regularly, and another 20% reported that their school has an induction program that is used regularly and has a positive impact on student learning.

While it is encouraging that nearly 70% of teachers are reporting that induction programs exist in their schools, there is clearly room to strengthen these programs and build additional programs in schools that do not have programs in place or do not use them to support new teachers.

Rewarding High-Performing Teachers

The systems that define teacher compensation typically operate outside the control of a particular school. Nevertheless, school leaders do have options for rewarding exceptional teacher performance. Incentives for teachers may include individual or group rewards. For example, at the individual level, school leaders could provide exceptional performers with additional opportunities to attend conferences, leadership opportunities, private acknowledgment (such as thank-you notes), and public recognition. Leaders may also recognize exceptional group performance by providing release time for effective teacher teams to conduct their work, additional professional development opportunities, acknowledgment of good work, and public recognition and celebrations.

In prior work, we found that expectancy theory, which explores why people make the choices they do, can help to explain teacher motivation.[4] In organizations, leaders need to set up rewards for desirable choices in ways that make sense to employees.[5] Motivating action in an organization requires that leaders understand actors' perceptions of organizational goals, that actors see the goals as achievable, and that the incentive system encourages goal achievement. Outcomes may include rewards like being part of a community, more money, public recognition, or a feeling of satisfaction. There may also be disincentives, such as the burden of extra work needed to pursue goals or reduced status and increased stress associated with failing to achieve a challenging goal. Aligning the reward system with desired behaviors is a key challenge of improving organizational practices from within.

Because schools require collaboration and trust between teachers to be effective, individual performance awards can undermine collaboration and trust among colleagues. For example, when schools reward a small number of teachers for improving individual test scores in their classrooms, they can develop a fragmented culture that pits teachers against one another to conceal the strategies that led to their success. Our research on pay for performance suggested that if the school is to succeed as a professional community, designing incentives that reward collective achievements is much better for reinforcing, rather than undermining, a collaborative school culture.[6]

The most effective schools may be those that design improvement goals around group performance and recognize and reward groups of teachers for effective collaborative work rather than singling out individuals for their exceptional performance. But in our data, the same percentage of schools, 64%, reported that they provide rewards and recognition for both individual and group performance.

We believe that additional creative thought needs to be invested in considering ways to effectively reward groups within schools. Consistent with the distributed leadership perspective, leadership is a characteristic of the organization, and an important component of leadership in schools is the leadership that emerges from the work of groups of teachers working together. Clear articulation of the expectations of groups and recognition and rewards for group production could provide an important motivating tool to encourage and reinforce this collaborative work.

Identifying and Addressing Poor Teacher Performance

Identifying and addressing the performance of teachers who struggle is important at every school. Key first steps are monitoring and identifying poor performance, diagnosing the cause, and creating a clear plan to address it. Poor performance may be due to a lack of training, a lack of motivation, a lack of clarity about work expectations, or a reflection of a temporary or chronic personal issue such as health, divorce, or caring for a family member. The focus on student learning priority can conflict with a community's commitment to take care of its own. Members of educator communities need to look out for one another in order to protect group members, but a narrative focused on student learning must be a priority when one of the group members is not contributing to the larger goal.

The capacity to address the needs of low-performing educators showed some of the widest gaps between leader and teacher perception the CALL survey. Over 75% of school leaders reported that teachers who struggle initially receive support to improve but then are counseled out, convinced to resign, or dismissed if they fail to improve. (Our data do not measure whether these teachers leave teaching or if they are simply transferred to another school in the district or to another district.) About 10% of leaders reported that low performers are simply allowed to continue to teach without support or intervention. Another small but significant group (15% for elementary schools, 10% for secondary schools) reported that low-performing teachers are shifted to another teaching assignment. In other words, most leaders report that problems of struggling teachers are handled effectively through remediation but then, if necessary, dismissal.

A much higher proportion of the teachers report that low-performing teachers are allowed to continue in their roles without support or intervention. About half of CALL teachers reported that they don't know how low performance is addressed in their school. Of the remainder, about a quarter believe that nothing happens to address poor performance (23% for elementary schools, 28% for secondary schools). It is worth noting that performance issues involve some element of confidentiality, so other teachers may not be aware that the supervisor is working with a low-performing teacher to help that person improve, counsel him or her, or dismiss him or her. We believe it is important for the school community to understand the process and have confidence that poor performance is taken seriously and is not allowed to continue.

4.2 STRUCTURING AND MAINTAINING TIME

- Is time for collaborative work allocated and used effectively?
- How are decisions made when designing teacher and student schedules?
- What factors are considered when deciding whether to provide a student with access to advanced-level course content?

Resource allocation often focuses on money. While financial resources are important, here we examine the leadership tasks that strategically align time with school improvement goals. By structuring teacher and student time to support learning, leaders create the conditions for teachers and students to succeed.

Time to Collaborate

In Chapter 5, we discussed the process of using collaborative design to create professional community. Leaders need to allocate sufficient time to engage in the kinds of professional interaction that create relational trust. About 75% of teachers report that school leaders provide shared time for them to plan curricula. This shared time supports teacher collaboration around student learning. Most teachers report that they use this time to talk with colleagues about goals for student learning. (Only about 1% of teachers report that they work on their own instead of participating in these meetings.) About 75% of teachers report that they meet to discuss student learning, and in that time, they develop formal strategies to address learning needs. While there is room for improvement, most teachers in most schools have dedicated collaborative time to work on instruction, and they report that they use this time to improve their practice.

Teacher and Student Scheduling

Teacher assignment to classes and responsibilities is an important resource allocation issue. Ideally, teachers are matched to courses primarily with student learning needs in mind. Putting a novice teacher in classrooms with challenging students all day serves neither the teacher nor the students. Schools can saddle new teachers with heavy loads to rid veteran teachers of undesirable classes.

Teachers in one urban school talked about avoiding investing in relationships with new teachers because they would probably be leaving soon. The strategy of loading up new and disempowered teachers with difficult assignments can serve the interests of veteran teachers, but it does not serve the interests of the students or the long-term health of the school community.

Teacher seniority has proven to be a powerful motive in shaping teacher assignment. In many schools, senior teachers are allowed to assign teaching loads for political as well as academic reasons. The practice of allowing senior teachers, such as department and area chairs, to designate assignments is deeply rooted in a loosely coupled culture where teachers are allowed to control the instructional domain. There are problems with creating schedules based on seniority, however. First, inexperienced teachers are in their learning years, and they are less likely to be effective with challenging assignments than senior colleagues. Second, new teachers faced with an overly demanding course load may not come back, creating a revolving door of new teachers in the school. About 10 years ago, one of us was interviewing high school teachers as part of a study. One new teacher had been given a heavy teaching load of the most undesirable courses in the school. She reported that she was struggling with how many preparations she was asked to carry. Her classes also seemed to have a high number of students who had difficulty in other classes, and although her senior colleagues seemed to have much lighter teaching loads, they had little time to observe and support her. The interview took place in the winter, and it was clear she would not be returning to that school the next year.

Teachers should be assigned to match their strengths to the greatest student learning needs. So while some attention to teacher workplace demands is important, teacher schedules ideally would be determined with the best interests of students in mind. Table 6.1 shows the percentage of teachers reporting that each criterion mattered "quite a bit" or "a great deal" in determining teacher assignment decisions in elementary and secondary schools. About half of the participating teachers reported that matching teacher skills to student learning

Table 6.1 Role of Expertise in Teaching Assignments

BASIS OF TEACHING ASSIGNMENTS	ELEMENTARY SCHOOL	MIDDLE OR HIGH SCHOOL
Teacher skills match learning needs	53%	52%
Teacher expertise in subject	60	75

Note: The table shows the percent of teachers reporting that the factor influenced the teaching assignment "quite a bit" or "a great deal."

needs or, in elementary schools, matching teaching skills to instructional design are important factors in shaping teacher assignment decisions. While it is a positive sign that fully half of teachers reported that teachers are assigned to classes based to a large extent on student learning needs, that still means that nearly half reported that assignments are made only somewhat (about 17%), a little (4% to 5%), or not at all (6% at the elementary level, 2% at the secondary level) based on student learning needs.

To the extent that teacher assignment is not made based on the needs of students, how are these decisions made? At the high school level, there tends to be more flexibility in assignment due to the larger number of courses offered within academic departments. About 15% of secondary school teachers reported that assignments were made to enable teachers to rotate through a desirable or undesirable assignment. About 11% of elementary teachers and 17% of secondary teachers identified seniority as an important predictor of assignment. Assignments based on seniority and rotation tend to reflect teacher-centered rather than student-centered leadership environments.

The effectiveness of the school depends on connecting teacher expertise to student learning needs. Schools that move learning forward pay careful attention to allocating human resources in ways that most effectively address the learning needs of students. An important leadership task therefore is to set up teacher assignments based primarily on student learning needs, so the very best teachers would be accessible to all types of students and not, for example, limited to students in advanced-level classes.

Another time allocation decision involves the assignment of students to classes. Research on student allocation of time suggests that students perform best when challenged in high-level classes with rigorous content. Yet many schools continue to block access to students from the most challenging learning opportunities. Thirty percent of elementary teachers and nearly 20% of high school teachers said that student course assignments were rarely or never made to maximize access for students to advanced courses and gifted and talented learning opportunities. Many teachers (35% elementary school and 23% middle and high school) didn't know how student course assignments were made. Furthermore, if the goal of school is to motivate students to want to learn, only 18% of middle and high school teachers said that their school determined placement of students into challenging classes based on the student's motivation or interest. The highest-ranking factor was teacher permission or recommendation (20.8%), which research has shown can limit access for students of color.[7]

Tracking, or ability grouping, provided another model that was widely used in CALL schools. Tracking selects groups of students based on similar perceived abilities to receive instruction calibrated to their learning level. Although this is a widely used strategy that provides a convenient way to reduce the variation of student learning needs in the classroom, it has been heavily criticized as a pernicious practice that reinforces the effects of segregation by denying low-achieving students access to peer communities and challenging courses they need to succeed.[8] In this model, students are grouped together at the same levels of learning so teachers can teach students with similar needs together. While this enables teachers to target their instruction, it also prevents lower-achieving and special needs students from having access to complex content and engagement of potentially more interesting materials in higher-level classes.[9]

4.3 SCHOOL RESOURCES FOCUS ON STUDENT LEARNING

- Are additional resources available during or after the school day for struggling students?
- Does the school have a process to ensure that all students have an opportunity to engage in extracurricular activities?
- Are school leaders successful in acquiring resources to support student learning?

A few years ago we had an opportunity to work with several high schools to build the instructional leadership capacity of their teachers. In a series of workshops, we asked teachers in those schools to tell us about the resources that were available to high-achieving, middle-level, and low-achieving students. In both districts, teachers reported that middle-level students were the target audience of instruction in the classroom, and they were primarily served through the core instructional programs. But the districts had different approaches to students at the ends of the achievement spectrum. In the low-performing district, schools targeted significant resources for remediation programs that would address the needs of students who struggled the most during the school day, after school, and in summers. In the high-performing district, the schools targeted significant resources to the highest performers in extracurricular activities where students could work with scientists, learn to fly a plane, or work with researchers in a museum, for example.

In our data, over 75% of teachers reported that their school had programs that offered additional instruction to struggling students. Only about a third of teachers, however, reported that these programs improved student learning. Elementary school teachers believed that the programming offered during the day was more effective, with about half of teachers reporting that targeted intervention periods during the school day improved learning for struggling students.

This distribution of supplemental learning resources is troubling for addressing the needs of all children. Low-performing, high-poverty students tend to get remediation in their extracurricular learning, while high-performing, low-poverty students get creative opportunities to express themselves in challenging domains. From a learning perspective, all children need opportunities to engage in adventurous learning. In fact, students who regularly receive the kinds of scripted literacy and math instruction that dominates high-poverty schools are most in need of enriching extracurricular learning they do not have access to at home.[10]

Because of the inequities we saw in our work with urban schools, we were interested in whether schools put in place processes to determine if extracurricular programs provide adequate opportunities to engage all students. Our data suggest that the attention to this problem is very limited. Fully half of teachers report there is no process in their school to examine who is participating in extracurricular programming; no efforts are being made to be sure the resources invested in extracurricular offerings are designed to engage all types of students in rich learning opportunities. While schools often have less control of the mandated curriculum they teach, they do have considerable control over the range of supplementary learning activities they can offer.

Expectancy theory suggests that if teachers don't believe they can achieve a goal (such as the belief that a new program will actually improve learning), they won't pursue it. From our data, 44% of elementary teachers and 58% of secondary teachers indicated that the lack of funding impeded pursuit of innovative programming. Administrators were slightly more optimistic but shared a similar view, with 38% of elementary administrators and 45% of secondary administrators indicating that the lack of funding was impeding innovation. While the research on school funding has shown mixed results in the ability of additional resources to improve learning outcomes, our analysis suggests that the lack of resources to support new initiatives is impeding innovation in support of student learning in many schools. As others have noted, it is not just the amount of resources but also how they are allocated that affect student learning outcomes.[11]

Some leaders actively seek material and human resources to complement the school's instructional program. In our schools, 23% of elementary teachers and 17% of secondary teachers reported that school leaders were very or extremely successful in acquiring funds for hiring new staff members (e.g., through grant writing or negotiations with the district). Schools that close achievement gaps and improve learning for all students seek to acquire and align financial resources with learning goals.[12]

4.4 INTEGRATING EXTERNAL EXPERTISE INTO THE SCHOOL INSTRUCTIONAL PROGRAM

- Do school leaders provide teachers with information and resources to improve teaching and learning?
- Do educators engage in online and in-person professional networks?
- Does the school reach out and integrate external expertise into the school community?

No school is an island of expertise. This is particularly relevant in today's information economy. Educators have never had such easy access to a rich array of professional learning communities and curricular resources. Leaders need to cultivate educator connections to these wider knowledge networks. They should know which networks the best teachers in the school join and provide incentives for all teachers to engage in such networks. Expert knowledge in the field of education is continually evolving. Schools monitor developments in the field, but they cannot be expected to be experts in new policies and instructional approaches. Therefore, an important role of school leaders is to provide school personnel access to knowledge and expertise to support school improvement. Common sources of this expertise are resources such as articles, external professional development opportunities, district experts, and external consultants.

Developing Teacher Expertise

An important way in which school leaders support bringing new knowledge into the school environment is by providing resources to teachers and supporting teachers in developing networks by attending professional conferences. Every state has professional organizations to serve educator interests across the disciplines: science, social studies, language learning, special education, learning technologies, and even rural and vocational education have professional associations in most states. Online communities like Pinterest and Google Groups draw hundreds of thousands of teachers to share and search for resources and advice.[13] Teachers who are not connected to professional networks are working at a disadvantage to their connected peers.

The best practices in this area are creating a formal process for sharing information when teachers return to the school so that the school as a whole can benefit from the advancement of an individual teacher. School leaders link staff with professional conferences and other resources so that these resources can be added to the school's intellectual capital and shared as appropriate with all staff. Electronic resources, including virtual learning options for teachers and students, are made available and appropriately woven in with existing program initiatives.

Schools vary greatly in their approaches to coordination of these external professional development opportunities. In some schools, teachers have significant discretion to decide what kinds of professional development they want to participate in. In the best schools, school leaders have established a process to coordinate participation and professional conferences and organizations to find new ideas for school improvement. In our sample, over half (55%) of the teachers reported that their school leaders prioritized these kinds of professional development opportunities to support teacher learning. A similar proportion of teachers indicated that their schools had a process in place for teachers to share information with other teachers after attending professional conferences, with 61.2% of elementary teachers and 58.3% of secondary teachers reporting that there was a process and it was actively used.

Tapping External Expertise

Learning to teach differently is a social activity. Simply reading about a change is seldom sufficient. Successful reform depends on working with experts who can provide ongoing feedback on the development of new practices. District experts and external consultants can bring needed expertise to the school to improve the quality of reformed practices. About three-quarters of the schools in our sample bring in district experts to support the needs of the school. The teachers in our sample view district experts as a more useful resource than external consultants because they have an understanding of problems in school and their work is more relevant to school needs. External consultants tend to have a more limited understanding of the local context, and their efforts may compete with rather than support school improvement.

A major challenge of managing external expertise is that experts often bring their own agenda into the school without an awareness of the school's history,

Table 6.2 Percentages of Teachers Reporting That District and External Experts Understand Their Needs and Provide Helpful Support to Improve the School

	HELPFUL	NOT HELPFUL
District experts	Elementary school: 49% Secondary school: 47%	Elementary school: 27% Secondary school: 26%
External experts	Elementary school: 40% Secondary school: 30%	Elementary school: 40% Secondary school: 41%

context, or expertise, and they fail to integrate new information into the existing instructional programs. Most teachers and administrators found the knowledge and information brought in by district experts and external consultants to provide important information that supported school improvement processes. But about 25% of teachers felt that district experts did not understand current problems in their school and their work was not relevant to school needs. An even higher percentage, 40% of teachers, felt that external experts (e.g., consultants) did not understand their needs and their work was not relevant to school needs (Table 6.2).

These data highlight the importance of working with outside consultants to ensure that they understand the school context and are providing support that advances rather than impedes school improvement. They suggest that external experts may provide more harm than good if not managed well. Schools that use external expertise effectively complement rather than compete with current expertise and programming.

4.5 COORDINATING AND SUPERVISING RELATIONS WITH FAMILIES AND EXTERNAL COMMUNITIES

- Does the school coordinate with social service agencies, churches, and other community organizations to offer opportunities for family engagement?
- Do school leaders schedule time and events convenient for families to discuss issues about schooling?
- Are educators encouraged to go beyond student-teacher conferences in building relationships with families?
- Are effective communication methods in place to inform parents about student performance?

A final leadership task related to resources in schools involves reaching out to family and community members to support student learning. Community resources can be very important, but these resources need to be targeted and directed to meaningfully support student learning. Outreach to community groups is a leadership task that is often sidelined in schools, but it can have far-reaching implications for student success. Well over half the teachers in our sample reported that their school did not have a process to coordinate with social service agencies, churches, or other community groups to provide learning opportunities outside school.

Similarly, schools vary in their ability to leverage parent and community support. Table 6.3 summarizes the data on parent attendance at parent-teacher conferences. When parents attend, 75 percent of teachers report that the resulting conversations are meaningful and focused on student work and student progress.

Outside of parent-teacher conferences, school leaders may also schedule informational meetings for teachers to talk to parents about student behavioral expectations, parent concerns, or curriculum and testing. At the elementary level, over 60% of elementary teachers and 50% to 60% of secondary teachers report that group meetings about student behavior and curriculum and testing are regularly scheduled. However, the communication more often flows from school to parent: over 50% of teachers report that they do not hold listening sessions in their schools to hear parent concerns.

Schools have systems in place to inform parents about problems with student attendance or performance, which schools consider to be somewhat to very effective. Public forums such as parent-teacher organization meetings, community dinners, or back-to-school nights are held about twice a year in secondary schools and three to five or more times per year in elementary schools. Elementary schools work harder to connect with family and community groups to determine the best time and location for public meetings. Few schools offer child care to support attendance.

Table 6.3 Parent Attendance at Parent-Teacher Conferences

	ELEMENTARY SCHOOL	SECONDARY SCHOOL
Low attendance	24.9%	40.8%
Moderate attendance	33.0	43.7
High attendance	37.0	14.1
Perfect attendance	5.1	1.4

The main concern with school efforts to establish relationships with communities is that simply announcing events rewards families with the time and social capital to participate. Middle-class families know that developing relationships with educators is an important way to advocate for the interests of their children. Poor families may not be able to make the time or may lack the transportation to take advantage of these opportunities. Furthermore, parents and guardians who are accustomed to interacting with professionals and experienced success in their own schooling assume an easy familiarity with educators. Parents who struggled in their own schooling or seldom interact with white-collar professionals may feel excluded at open-invitation school gatherings. Schools need to work harder to make disenfranchised families feel welcome in the school. At a minimum, schools need to provide transportation to important events. To fully integrate families in need into the school community, educators need to reach out to develop relationships with family members. Calling families when students struggle and directly communicating opportunities for engagement can transform a family on the fringe into a community member of the school.

PUTTING IT ALL TOGETHER: ACQUIRING AND ALLOCATING RESOURCES

This chapter has considered a number of areas of practice that leaders need to address to improve student learning. From a distributed leadership perspective, they need to acquire and allocate resources to establish the conditions of improving teaching and learning for all students. This means structuring ongoing interactions in ways that allocate space and resources to support best practices. Over time, these structures can shape routines that come to define organizational culture. Here we recommend several core practices that can become transformational routines in schools.

Inducting new faculty and making sure that faculty who struggle have opportunities to learn define subdomain 4.1. To support practices for inducting and managing personnel, CALL recommends:

- Making teacher assignments based on the match between the expertise of the teacher and the learning needs of students, making sure that all students have access to the strongest teachers.
- Setting clear goals and rewarding (through recognition, release time for focused work, conference opportunities, and other monetary or

nonmonetary rewards) groups of teachers who perform particularly well as a team.

- Creating clear guidelines for work expectations and addressing low performance by communicating and following a clear process to support low-performing teachers to improve their performance. For employees who fail to improve, establish clear procedures to counsel out or dismiss low-performing employees.

Subdomain 4.2 addresses the critical issue of structuring time to provide high-quality opportunities for faculty and student interaction. We know that relational trust grows when people ask for and receive help on problems that matter (see Chapter 5). Loosening up the schedule to find time for these kinds of interactions for both teachers and students increases the possibility of developing relational trust through the school. Structuring time also applies to the organization of teacher and student schedules and to ensuring that the most talented teachers work with students in greatest need of support. We recommend the following practices for structuring time effectively:

- Design inclusive groupings of students that include the full range of learning abilities and styles.
- Provide access to high-level courses to all students who are interested and motivated to work in these courses. Avoid using strategies such as teacher recommendations and course prerequisites that block student access to higher-level courses.
- Close the loop in planning by providing time for teachers to meet and talk about goals for student learning, develop formal strategies to address learning needs, and provide opportunities and accountability for implementation of these plans and ongoing reflection on their effectiveness.

Schools can no longer afford to rest on the expertise within the building. Leaders must create and reward pathways for teachers to participate in professional networks, whether in person or online, and bring their insights back into the school community. Enacting the practices of subdomain 4.3 leads us to recommend that leaders:

- Create adventurous learning opportunities to engage students who struggle with supplementary activities that expand their horizons.
- Evaluate your school's program to ensure that the needs of all students are served by the core classroom experience, and extracurricular activities

support the engagement, motivation, and activation of learning for all students, not just a small subset of the school population.

- Invite and provide support for teachers to participate in an online and an in-person professional network. Create structured opportunities for teachers to share their experiences with like-minded colleagues and with the faculty broadly.

- Select external experts who can develop the kinds of long-term relationships with school staff that result in ongoing feedback and learning. Familiarize experts with current issues and problems facing the school and with the strategies the school is already undertaking to improve student learning.

In an era where school funding is a perennial topic of public budget shortfalls, resourceful school leaders must look to alternative sources of support for new initiatives. However, taking support from groups with agendas of their own risks diverting school attention from their shared commitment to goals for school improvement. Leaders should continue to seek these kinds of supports and at the same time reconcile the shared goals of the school with the mission of external partners. For subdomain 4.4, we offer these recommendations:

- When making resource allocation decisions, including routine decisions that have been in place, consider what value this activity is adding to the school community. Are all students being served by the activity? Are there better ways to design the activity to engage, motivate and support the learning of all students?

Finally, most schools need to do a better job of facilitating interaction with local communities. Simply holding events is not enough to overcome the social capital gaps some families perceive as an obstacle for participation. Instead, school leaders must reach out by encouraging educators to develop relationships with families who may feel marginalized in the school community. To support these practices in subdomain 4.5, we suggest that school leaders:

- Evaluate which community groups are in the best position to engage students and families who have limited participation in the school community. Think about how these groups can support engagement and enrichment activities. Create a process to work with community groups to support student development needs.

- Provide support for teachers to make parent-teacher communications meaningful and focused on helping students succeed academically. Create incentives and motivate parents to participate in parent meetings and parent-teacher conferences.

Putting these resources into play can create the time, opportunities for learning, and relationships necessary to engage students and families in the learning process.

In the next chapter, we turn to the heart of the school's ability to engage students: the design of the learning environment. Inequities in the space where learning happens can undermine the best efforts of professional community and relationships to guide teaching and learning. In Chapter 7, we examine how educators can create an environment for learning as a place where all the CALL practices can take effect.

NOTES

1. Cavanagh, S. (2011, January 5).
2. Ingersoll, R. (2012); Ingersoll, R., & May, H. (2011); Ingersoll, R., & Perda, D. (2010).
3. Ingersoll. (2012, p. 50).
4. Odden, A., & Kelley, C. (2002).
5. Vroom, V. H., & Deci, E. L. (1983).
6. Kelley, C., Heneman, H. G. III, & Milanowski, A. (2002).
7. Cross, C. T., & Donovan, M. S. (Eds.). (2002).
8. For a review of the equity issues involved in tracking, see Gamoran, A. (2009). Research on the limits of tracking has led to a flourishing research and practice community around differentiation that addresses the needs of diverse learners in the regular classroom context. See Tomlinson, C. A. (1999). As we shall see in Chapter 7, the recent dominance of response to intervention models in special education, which sort all students into three tiers and then often address the needs of students who struggle in separate settings, has had the effect of reintroducing problems associated with tracking back into the policy mainstream.
9. Ruijs, N. M., & Peetsma, T. T. (2009).
10. Connected learning provides a rationale and several compelling models for how to engage disenfranchised youth in compelling learning with new media. For a discussion of this exciting work, see Ito, M., et al. (2013).
11. Miles, K. H., & Frank, S. (2008).
12. Kelley, C. J., & Shaw, J. J. (2009).
13. Halverson, R., Kallio, J., Hackett, S., & Halverson, E. (2016).

Domain 5: Establishing a Safe and Effective Learning Environment

| 1 Focus on Learning | 2 Monitoring Teaching & Learning | 3 Professional Community | 4 Acquiring & Allocating Resources | 5 Safe & Effective Environment |

	DOMAIN 5: ESTABLISHING A SAFE AND EFFECTIVE LEARNING ENVIRONMENT	TOTAL	ELEMENTARY	SECONDARY	LEADERS
		3.4	3.4	3.4	3.5
5.1	Clear, consistent, and enforced expectations for student behavior	3.7	3.7	3.6	3.9
5.2	Clean and safe learning environment	3.5	3.4	3.5	3.5
5.3	Support services for students who traditionally struggle	3.1	3.0	3.0	3.2

Note: Five-point scale. $N=18,677$ respondents.

T HE CHALLENGE OF ESTABLISHING A SAFE AND EFFECTIVE LEARNING SPACE
for all students has become the arena where socially and culturally contested
norms for appropriate behavior have played out in schools. Nearly all
educators, students, and families agree that safe and effective learning spaces
are essential. Developing and consistently enforcing behavioral standards for
all students is an important feature of safe learning environments, and effective
programs such as response to intervention that design learning to meet student
needs are important to engage all learners. However, the implementation of
these kinds of efforts to ensure these spaces are safe and effective has resulted
in unanticipated side effects that can disproportionally punish some students
and segregate others into separate learning spaces. The leadership challenge for
schools today is to create safe and effective learning environments that include all
students and motivate them to engage in their own learning.

This chapter considers the core tasks in building the kinds of learning
environments that support learning for all students. American Federation of
Teachers president Randi Weingarten recently noted:

> The discipline policies of the past that emphasize punishment over
> developing positive behaviors are not working. As well-meaning as they were,
> they have made our schools more inequitable. We now have a chance to learn
> from these mistakes. We can, and we must, do better for all our kids.[1]

What does it mean to "do better for all our kids"? What can we learn from what
we were doing in schools, and where can leaders turn to establish safe and
effective learning environments while meeting the challenge of educating all
students? In CALL Domain 5, we engage in a discussion that describes practices to
meet Weingarten's challenge. We review the items and responses in this domain
to get a better sense of what kinds of practices are in use for building safe learning
environments. We then explore several of the leading directions for future action
on creating safe and effective learning environments. We discuss how programs
designed to address the consequences and causes of student behavior, such as
positive behavioral interventions and supports and restorative justice models, can
establish safe spaces for all students to thrive.

THE PRACTICES THAT MATTER TO DEVELOP SAFE AND EFFECTIVE LEARNING ENVIRONMENTS

The challenge to provide safe and effective learning environments has traditionally revolved around two key issues. First, schools are responsible for developing standards that encourage students to behave fairly toward one another by discouraging (and punishing) inappropriate behaviors. Second, schools are responsible for using the tools and resources of student services (e.g., special education, talented and gifted education, English language learning programs) to provide appropriate services for students who struggle in regular classroom settings.

These two levels of support, schoolwide policies and student-specific initiatives, form a complex network of tools and practices leaders can use to create safe and effective learning for all students. In schools that work well, students and teachers establish norms for fair and inclusive environments in which all students receive the supports they need to succeed. In schools that struggle, unfairly enforced behavioral policies disproportionately target students with special needs, who are then excluded from the regular classroom experience. Students who need the most help to succeed in school can end up being targeted as obstacles for establishing a safe and effective learning environment.

The challenge to provide safe learning environments must not be met at the cost of disproportionate enforcement of behavioral standards for students. As Daniel Losen and his colleagues powerfully suggest, "If we ignore the discipline gap, we will be unable to close the achievement gap."[2] It falls to leaders to put in place practices to provide safe, fair, and effective learning environments for all students. Managing the complex balance of these two priorities requires constant attention.

Because many of the regulations that support services for student behavior and disabilities come with legal sanctions and restrictions, managing the tangle can become a gauntlet for many leaders to avoid litigation rather than a resource for supporting desired outcomes. Since the policy tools of special education and school safety often require specialized knowledge and skill, the exercise of these tools can define a small group of leaders as the gatekeepers of special services. Leaders interested in using these tools to work toward schoolwide goals for behavior and learning must break out of the trap of specialized knowledge and skill to include all educators in schoolwide and student-level supports.

In the following sections, we discuss educator responses to these practices in the context of the wider discussion of key research on school safety issues. The CALL survey invites feedback from educators around three key tasks for building safe and effective learning environments:

	DOMAIN	CORE PRACTICES
5.1	Clear, consistent, and enforced expectations for student behavior	Everyone in the school is engaged in modeling and supporting students to behave in terms of shared expectations. The school provides opportunities for teachers to regularly review student discipline data and address inequities as they arise.
5.2	Clean and safe learning environment	Schools promote student learning by respecting students and teachers through maintenance of clean and safe hallways, bathrooms, classrooms, libraries, cafeterias, and school grounds.
5.3	Student services for students who traditionally struggle	Systems are established to ensure that all students receive the help they need before they are allowed to fail. Educators regularly evaluate data to refine the effectiveness of classroom teaching and intervention strategies.

The story of leadership efforts to provide appropriate behavioral and special education services in schools is complex. In the following sections, we consider how the histories of the efforts to provide appropriate supports for students who struggle has resulted in whole-school reform initiatives. We begin with a consideration of how behavior policies rooted in zero-tolerance initiatives in the 1990s have resulted in the disproportionate exclusion of students of color from regular classroom environments. We then consider how special education policies designed to address the needs of all students resulted in reinforcing the kinds of in-school segregation they were designed to avoid. We conclude the chapter by pointing toward the kinds of new initiatives developed by schools to guarantee a safe learning environment for all students while effectively providing services for students who struggle the most to succeed in school.

5.1 CLEAR, CONSISTENT, AND ENFORCED EXPECTATIONS FOR STUDENT BEHAVIOR

- Does the discipline policy for students in the school focus on the benefits of positive behavior, and is it integrated into everyday interaction?
- How consistently do school staff members enforce student discipline policies for all students?

- How well do school community members understand the school's expectations for student behavior?

The key pivot in recent discussions about school safety sits in the space between articulating and enforcing expectations for student behavior. As we noted, leaders need to create environments that protect students while at the same time preventing the unfair application of policies.

Schools are eager to put policies and practice in place to ensure that students can learn (and teachers can teach) in safe spaces. Researchers have long shown that a safe learning environment is an essential support for successful school learning. Disruptive student behavior undermines teaching efforts and diverts educator attention away from teaching and learning and into behavior management.[3] Classroom management practices that emphasize order and appropriate behavior are critical conditions for improving student outcomes.[4] Elaine Allensworth and her colleagues documented that establishing a safe learning environment, combined with expectations for high achievement, is among the most important tasks of school leadership. James Sebastian and Allensworth found that establishing a strong school culture and climate are the strongest leadership practices for improving learning in high schools.[5] Even schools with strong teachers struggle to improve learning when the school is perceived as unsafe.[6]

Every year schools across the country spend millions of dollars on people and programs to create safe learning environments. The central goal for building a safe learning environment is to establish agreed-on and fairly enforced codes that define appropriate behavior for students and adults in schools and define and implement consequences for not following the codes. Many schools work out a manageable relationship between expectations and behavior to create a safe learning environment. In the CALL survey, 70% of educators reported that the enforcement of school policies helped to create a safe learning environment. Building and implementing behavior policies is such a central part of leadership that most schools establish a separate professional track, such as a dean of students or an assistant principal of student affairs or student services, to develop and enforce behavior policies ranging from attendance to expulsion.

The difficulty of creating a balance between policy and enforcement is also reflected in the CALL data. The first line in the effort to create a safe learning environment is to establish and follow fair behavioral standards. While 60% of educators felt that their school policies created a safe learning environment, only 28% felt that their discipline policies were very effective at eliminating disruptive behavior, and fewer than half (46%) felt that policies allowed educators to address behavioral concerns in a timely manner. Only 42% of CALL educators felt that staff in their schools consistently and regularly enforced discipline policies.

The precarious balance that schools struggle to find between developing and enforcing policies fairly is rooted in the recent history of policy evolution. The focus of school behavior policies has shifted considerably over the past 20 years.[7] In the 1980s and 1990s, there was widespread concern about the rise of youth violent behavior and crime in and out of schools. Between 1980 and 1994, the violent crime arrest rate for juveniles rose 60% and the murder arrest rate 100%.[8] These trends were felt more acutely in impoverished schools. In response, schools adopted more stringent disciplinary policies to control the day-to-day lives of students and teachers. Inspired by "broken windows" policies in criminology that the prevention of small violations would create an environment of safety to prevent major violations, the new wave of education policies emphasized mandatory punishments for a wide variety of offenses, a reliance on suspension and expulsion as consequences, and the increased involvement of police in the school building to enforce small infractions as a prevention for larger problems.[9]

The resulting ideas, called zero-tolerance policies, came to dominate discussions of leadership for safe and effective learning environments. Zero tolerance aims to reduce the discretion of local educators for imposing consequences for student behavior. It suggests that schools are made safe by removing problem students and that problem students can be either permanently kept apart from their peers or in some cases remediated to return to school but tracked into parallel classroom settings. By 1997, 79% of schools in the country had zero-tolerance policies.[10]

Over the first decade of the 21st century, schools gradually became aware of the costs of knitting together armed security guards, criminal justice officials, special educators, and school leaders to enforce high-stakes disciplinary policies.[11] Consequently, zero-tolerance policies have come under considerable attack, and many researchers and educators have begun to focus on their costs.

Researchers found that these kinds of policies resulted in a dramatic increase in the number of students suspended and expelled from schools. Jacob and colleagues report that by 2012, 2 million students were suspended from school every year, as compared with 3 million high school graduates each year.[12] A groundbreaking 2011 study in Texas, *Breaking Schools' Rules* by Tony Fabelo and his colleagues, documented the costs of no-excuses disciplinary policies:

- Over half of Texas students were suspended from school at some time.
- Almost one-third of all students had out-of-school suspensions.
- Nearly 15% of students were assigned to alternative education settings, and almost 10% ended up in juvenile justice programs.

The Texas study documented how the burden of zero tolerance fell disproportionately on students of color and students in special education:

- Eighty-three percent of all African American male students in Texas had at least one disciplinary violation compared with 74% of Latino males and 59% of white males.
- Nearly 75% of students in special education were suspended or expelled. Students labeled with an "emotional disturbance" were much more likely to be punished than students labeled with low-incidence disabilities such as blindness or autism.

Finally, the practice of pulling students from the common classroom harmed academic performance and set up a pathway to criminal behaviors:

- Thirty-one percent of suspended or expelled students repeated a grade compared with 5% of other students.
- Fifteen percent of students in Texas were involved with the juvenile justice system. Nearly half of students who were disciplined more than 10 times were in contact with juvenile justice compared with 2% of students with no disciplinary records.
- A student who was suspended or expelled was nearly three times more likely to become involved with the juvenile justice system the following year.[13]

Zero-tolerance policies initially aimed at restricting the discretion of local educators to impose punishments for student behavior. However, researchers found that the emphasis on strict rule enforcement expanded, rather than contracted, the ability of local educators to develop new approaches of using harsh enforcement of school policies to punish students. Locally defined categories such as "insubordination" or "willful defiance" described a majority of the disciplinary actions taken by educators across the nation. In California, for example, nearly half of the 700,000 suspensions in the 2011–12 school year were labeled as "willful defiance";[14] nationally, 43% of expulsions and out-of-school suspensions were labeled as some form of insubordination.[15] Remarkably, the *Breaking Schools' Rules* researchers found that only 3% of suspensions and expulsions were for severe offenses that required mandatory consequences—which meant that 97% of punishments were prescribed at the discretion of educators.

The consequences of zero-tolerance policies have disproportionately punished a generation of young people as the cost of preserving school safety. Decoteau Irby has shown how school discipline codes have evolved to get students into deeper trouble more quickly.[16] The benefit of these policies for establishing safe learning environments is also in question. Jacob Kang-Brown and his colleagues highlight the absence of research to show a positive relation between exclusionary discipline and the reduction of student disruptions in classrooms.[17] John Hoffman, Lance Erickson, and Karen Spence explored the relation of student misbehavior, suspension, and academic outcomes. They found that excluding students from classrooms is the consequence of high-stakes disciplinary policies.[18] Exclusion has created a generation of young people who do not benefit from schooling and struggle to find a viable place in society.

These patterns of disproportional effects of school disciplinary policies were reflected in the CALL data as well. The CALL survey found that:

- Fifty-seven percent of CALL educators felt that staff in their school disciplined male students more than they did females.
- Seventy-one percent felt that students of color were disciplined more heavily than other students.
- Seventy percent felt that students from low-income families received more discipline.
- Seventy-five percent felt that students with learning disabilities received more discipline than other students.
- Eighty-six percent felt that English language learning students received more disciplinary action than other students.

One way to interpret the inequitable results of policy enforcement is to examine whether educators adequately understand the policies. Nearly three-quarters of CALL educators felt that administrators, teachers, and staff understood policies well. Half of the educators felt that they had developed a system that successfully guided student conduct by focusing on positive behaviors. To share a common understanding of the system, nearly half of CALL educators reported meeting at least monthly to discuss issues with student behavior. Discussions about student behavior and the relation of the school's disciplinary policy to student action form a central opportunity for interaction in building relational trust in many schools.

The same educators, however, said that only 56% of students understood expectations for behavior and only 37% of parents understood behavioral expectations very well. This clearly points to an opportunity for action in working with parents and students to come to a shared understanding of behavioral expectations for all students. Inviting interactions when behavioral policies are violated is probably not the best time to developing shared understandings. For students who are selected for action, the interactions may be characterized by resistance and a dispute over the reasons or the consequences of the action. When compounded by misunderstandings due to the disproportional application of discipline, it is difficult to see how these interactions could regularly result in relational trust.

The mismatch between the seemingly "fair" expressed policies of integrated schools and the unfair application of these policies is explored in Amanda Lewis and John Diamond's book, *Despite the Best Intentions: Why Racial Inequality Thrives in Good Schools.*[19] Their book summarizes five years of research in a diverse suburban school to explore how racial difference shapes the school policy development and implementation process. Lewis and Diamond traced the day-to-day interactions of students and teachers on typical school days and found that policies that were framed to address the behavior of all students were being used to disproportionately punish the behavior of students of color. They noted that both black and white students said that black students would be asked for hall passes or would be cautioned to be quiet, while similar interactions seldom happened for white students. Teachers tended to view white students, by default, as academically capable, while frequently expressing reservations about the academic abilities of black students. Lewis and Diamond uncovered a paradoxical world in which students, teachers, and parents realized that the policies were designed to work for all students while at the same time understanding that the implementation of these policies was unfair.

In Chapter 5, we discussed the relation of espoused theories and theories-in-action in professional learning. Unless learning engages educators' theories-in-action, professionals can continue to literally say one thing and do another. Making theories-in-action public creates an authentic opportunity to change behaviors. By situating research at the level of the day-to-day practice of educators and students, Lewis and Diamond provide an excellent example of how to display the contrast between intentions and actions that can reshape practices to create more equitable application of school discipline policies. Later in this chapter, we consider two leading approaches, positive behavioral intervention systems and restorative justice, as pathways for action once the discrepancies between policy and practice are on the table.

5.2 CLEAN AND SAFE LEARNING ENVIRONMENT

- How has the school conducted and used sources of information to set and evaluate progress toward meeting goals for improving student learning?
- How do leaders, educators, students, and the community work together to provide a safe and clean learning environment?

Successful learning takes place in spaces where students feel valued and safe. Schools that promote student learning respect students and teachers by maintaining clean and safe hallways, bathrooms, classrooms, libraries, cafeterias, and school grounds. Student assemblies are well managed and often involve student leadership in planning and carrying out community gatherings. The model school values and protects the learning environment by protecting learning time from interruptions by loudspeaker announcements or other distractions.

The need for a clean, well-tended learning environment in schools is reflected in research in establishing safe public spaces through community policing. Safety is an aspect of both physical and social spaces. The cleanliness of physical spaces is a sign that educators care about the conditions for teaching and learning. As might be expected, educators in CALL schools varied widely about their perceptions of the cleanliness of school conditions. Respondents felt that libraries were the cleanest and safest spaces in the school and that buses were the worst. On a school-by-school basis, this information could indicate where school leaders must act.

Safety in social spaces reflects the quality of interpersonal interaction in the school. For many educators, student behavior was a frequent disruption to the learning environment. Forty-two percent of respondents felt that student behavior disturbed the classroom very often, and 48% felt that such behavior always disrupted the learning environment. Twenty percent of CALL educators said that student disruptions of classrooms happened daily. These indicators of student disruption invite leaders and teachers to explore the reasons for and consequences of student disruption.

As with the Lewis and Diamond study, studying patterns and reports of disruptive behaviors can reveal opportunities for the school community to tackle theories-in-action on a pathway to a safer learning environment. Irby suggests that we think of school discipline policies in terms not of desired behaviors but of "balancing and managing complex, differentiated systems of trouble."[20] Irby "does not regard getting in trouble or punishment as inherently negative."[21] Rather, he asks educators (and researchers) to attend to the systems of control, or "social discipline nets," that use minor disciplinary violations as a pathway to involvement with counselors, psychologists, and, ultimately, law enforcement and legal authorities. If the espoused theory is school safety, then the theory-in-action is placement of students in the social discipline net. Irby's work challenges us to rethink the question of safe learning environment by presenting students an ascending ladder of consequences. While these kinds of policies may address the needs of most students and teachers, Irby reminds us that if the price is turning a small number of students into criminals, the cost is too high.

5.3 SUPPORT SERVICES FOR STUDENTS WHO TRADITIONALLY STRUGGLE

- How effective are support services for advancing student learning?
- How does the school's response to intervention program affect instruction for students?
- How many students progress out of support programs for students who struggle into the regular education program?

CALL Domain 5.3 describes the practices of student services providers, classroom teachers, administrators, and community members who work to address the needs of students struggling with the regular education program. Public schools have an obligation to guarantee equitable access to learning opportunities to students who traditionally struggle in schools. Providing safe and effective learning spaces for these students has meant developing programs to identify and build learning plans for students with learning disabilities or emotional behavioral disabilities and English language learners.

The responsibility to provide equitable access to learning for all students has come to define the mission of public schools. The evolution of this mission, however, has left behind a formidable and sometimes confusing tangle of policies and procedures for educators to navigate in order to serve the needs of all students. Creating learning opportunities for all students relies on tools and ideas developed across the complex history of special education.

The story of this legacy begins in the 1950s with the national struggle to overcome racial segregation in schools. Prior to the epochal 1954 *Brown v. Board of Education* decision, local communities were required to provide access to public schooling for all children. This, of course, did not mean that all children would have access to the same quality of schools. Racial and class-based segregation meant that different children would attend schools with very different resources. The *Brown* decision called into question the importance of access with the decision that "separate educational facilities are inherently unequal." Prior to 1954, segregation was a key strategy to organize public schools. Districts could have separate schools for students of color or students with disabilities to preserve traditional school services for majority-culture students and families. After *Brown*, simply providing access to public schools was no longer adequate; now districts had to consider the quality of the educational experience as well as access.

Since the *Brown* decision, the meaning of providing equal access to quality education has evolved through a number of policy initiatives. In the 1960s, for example, a key feature of the Johnson administration's War on Poverty was to radically increase federal funding for education. The rationale was that federal investment could supplement unequal allocation of local resources, especially for communities that needed more help. Whereas the Great Society programs of the 1960s targeted primarily race and poverty differences in education, the 1970s saw significant legislation to address the needs of students with disabilities. The Education for All Handicapped Children Act of 1975 established the right to public education for all children regardless of disability, and the Individuals with Disabilities Education Act (IDEA) of 1990 declared that states that accept public funds for education must provide special education services. These landmark federal actions from 1954 to 1990 reframed the scope of public education in the United States. The new policies provided regulations and resources for schools to create high-quality education opportunities for all students.

These new policies directed public education toward new horizons of educational opportunity, but they also led to a number of troubling unanticipated consequences. First, the tools provided to guide the new practices create a dense bureaucratic tangle that required specialists to translate the promise of the new polices into quality practices. IDEA, for example, provided the Individualized Education Plan (IEP) as a process for customizing a learning plan for students who struggled. The development and maintenance of IEPs emphasized the roles of new professional specialists, such as school psychologists and special educators, into the everyday school community. As more students were assigned to IEPs, the specialists began to serve as gatekeepers to access the resources described in the laws. The requirement to comply with the bureaucratic aspects of the regulations, paired with the real risk of legal action by parents who felt inadequately served by the school, led to a cautious, legalistic climate around programs to support students with the greatest needs.

Second, the policies designed to reduce segregated service delivery often resulted in reproducing segregation in different forms. The advent of comprehensive public high schools in the 1960s, for example, typically included complex ability-based tracking systems that reproduced segregation inside the school. Special educators assigned students with IEPs to tracks outside the regular classrooms through pullout programs. As Hugh Mehan, Jane Mercer, and Robert Rueda observed, educators began to adapt policies designed to provide high-quality education experiences for all students to reproduce the previous routines of segregation—this time inside schools.[22]

Educators began to speak of inclusion and differentiation to mitigate the segregating effects of pullout programs. Inclusion was a movement to bring all students into the regular classroom for instruction. The 1990 IDEA law mandated that special education students should receive services in the "least restrictive" education spaces available. Advocates of inclusion built on this mandate to argue that the benefit of learning with peers improves the education of all students. Even when full inclusion is not possible, inclusive educators sought to minimize the role of pullout services or the use of resource rooms to address the needs of students with disabilities. Differentiation is an instructional strategy for teachers to address the needs of diverse groups of students within the regular classroom. In a differentiated classroom, all students aim toward the same learning goals, while the instructional tasks of the teacher vary according to established student needs. Taken together, inclusion and differentiation became two pillars of a movement to create more equitable learning environments for all students.

The No Child Left Behind (NCLB) Act of 2001 changed the conversation once more by focusing on public reporting of the outcomes of education. NCLB required that, to receive federal funding, all states needed to establish shared content standards and assessments that measured student performance in terms of these standards. Schools that did not produce evidence of adequate yearly progress in student test scores faced a menu of increasingly serious consequences. A key aspect of NCLB was the requirement that the outcome measures be provided for all students, including special education students and English language learners. Schools could no longer hide inadequate results by keeping performance data internal because all achievement scores were now on public display. Schools scrambled to redesign approaches that clearly failed to address the needs of students who struggled in schools and gave rise to a national discussion about what educators and policymakers could do about a persistent achievement gap.

The landscape of practices public school leaders use to provide services for students who traditionally struggle is defined by every aspect of this 70-year legacy. All public schools are required to provide special education services. Because the needs of individual students vary, each school needs trained professionals to assess student needs, develop appropriate plans, coordinate meetings with parents and teachers to refine and approve plans, and monitor student progress. All of these practices need to take place in the context of inclusive education environments in which special educators and classroom teachers work together to differentiate instruction according to defined student needs. Also, because the requirement that all students receive appropriate services is a federal regulation, school leaders must always be aware of the potential for legal action. When we consider that 13% of all public school students receive special education services[23] and that 9% of students receive services as English language learners,[24] it is little wonder that providing appropriate services is a huge investment in time and resources for public school leaders across the country.

The contemporary model of providing services for students who struggle is being reshaped by response to intervention (RtI). The Individuals with Disabilities Improvement Act of 2004 introduced RtI as a strategy to bring together the pieces of services for students who struggle into the accountability era. RtI is a data-rich, evidence-based approach that includes procedures for identifying appropriate services for students and three tiers of intervention that are designed to provide high-quality learning opportunities to catch students before they fail:

- *Catching students before they fail.* One of the long-standing critiques of traditional special education was that students had to fail in the traditional classroom in order to qualify for an IEP. RtI is instead organized around a universal screening model in which all children are assessed and monitored in terms of grade-level performance through ongoing data collection. The kinds of assessment data collected on an as-needed basis for students in the pre-NCLB era became standard practice for all students in RtI. Frank Gresham contrasts a deficit- versus risk-based approach to providing services. Deficit models depend on documenting a record of failure to determine the need for services, whereas risk models assess all children in order to avoid the damaging time waiting for a student to fail.[25]

- *Evidence-based curriculum.* RtI is built around the idea of evidence-based curriculum and instructional practices. Schools are encouraged to implement programs that are shown to improve learning for all students by rigorous evaluation practices. Each school is responsible for selecting evidence-based interventions to shape the core instructional program to meet the needs of all students.

- *Tiers of intervention.* Instead of customizing a unique program for each student who struggles, RtI calls for a tier-based model where all students receive support to succeed in the schoolwide program. Most students (around 80%) are categorized as tier 1 students, who participate in the regular evidence-based schoolwide curriculum. About 15% are tier 2 students, who struggle to make progress with peers in the regular classroom, and receive supplemental services, and about 5% of students are in tier 3, where many students receive the kinds of IEPs that characterize special education.

RtI models have transformed how schools think about special education. As Richard Allington notes, the law allows for schools to "take up to 15% of current special education allocation and use that money to prevent the development of learning or reading disabilities."[26] Many schools use RtI as a model for whole-school instructional design. RtI envelops the issues of inclusion, differentiation, service provision, and data-driven accountability into a massive national movement toward a common education model for all students. In a 2011 survey of 1,400 educators, 68% said that their districts implemented RtI and that the RtI has led to a decline in the number of students in special education.[27] Over 75% of CALL secondary educators and nearly 90% of elementary educators, reported that they have adopted RtI practices in their schools. No public school leader can ignore the role that RtI plays in shaping the contemporary conversation about how to provide services for students who struggle.

Any time an initiative like RtI gains widespread acceptance, the education community begins to reflect on its basic assumptions and how it fits with other education values:

- *Effects of RtI.* Researchers have not been able to definitively answer the question about the effectiveness of RtI. Like many other national movements in education, the variation in how RtI is implemented makes it difficult to accurately trace the actual effects of the intervention. Many small, controlled studies show the positive effects of RtI on early reading skills.[28] However, one recent federal study that used a national sample of 1,200 schools did not find any positive results for RtI. Instead, the researchers found that first graders who received tier 2 and 3 reading interventions did worse than students who did not receive the interventions and that students who already had IEPs did not catch up to their peers in RtI.[29]

- *Limitations of RtI.* The RtI instructional model emphasizes the dominance of recent education policies around standardizing education environments for students who struggle around the kinds of evidence-based practices that seem to flourish in high-poverty schools and are increasingly being abandoned in schools with the ability to include more choices for students and families.[30] RtI requires all students to learn the same content and outcomes, and such approaches can ignore the interests of students for determining their own learning outcomes.[31] The reliance on remediation as the key instructional strategy for students to "catch up" to peers can cease to motivate young people who may be more motivated by peer affiliation and following their own interests than in making up ground. RtI's reliance on common assessment measures and instructional contexts for all students also ignores the differences in the cultural worlds students and families bring to the classroom. By focusing on assessment data and culturally neutral interventions, RtI promotes a view of the learning world that overlooks the social and language resources critical for many students and families.[32]

Preserving school safety means adopting and enforcing fair discipline policies for all students. It requires building safe spaces where teachers and students can work together to achieve learning goals and also establishing spaces where all students have access to the resources and support they need to improve. As we have seen, students who struggle most in schools are often the victims of these policies, and the needs of these same students are often addressed in continuously evolving special education and English language learning programs that place considerable pressure on school leaders to guide appropriate implementation. Leaders must constantly work to balance protecting the learning environment for all students while using the considerable policy and system resources to address the needs of the most vulnerable learners. The CALL survey provides valuable feedback to school leaders in understanding the best practices to achieve this balance.

In the following section, we turn to some innovative new directions in helping educators satisfy all of these design goals.

PUTTING IT ALL TOGETHER: INNOVATIVE PRACTICES FOR BUILDING SAFE AND EFFECTIVE LEARNING ENVIRONMENTS

The legacy of zero tolerance, high-stakes accountability, and special education policies has opened up a vibrant design space for some educators interested in exploring the next frontier of learning environment design. New designs focus on the key insight discussed in Chapter 5 that developing relational trust is the key to a strong learning environment. Schools that implement behavioral policies onto students fail to engage learners in building the learning environment. Zero tolerance, high-stakes accountability, and special education all provide services for students without engaging students as partners in creating a shared, safe learning space. Schools have developed programs that extend data-driven decision making to student behavior management and build culturally responsive approaches that focus on peer and family relations to address student behavior. These kinds of programs use information, identity, peer relations, and culture to encourage students to participate in a strong school culture rather than focusing on the consequences for nonparticipation. In the final part of this section, we consider approaches to school safety grounded in creating trust through interactions among teachers, students, and content in classrooms.

Positive Behavioral Interventions and Supports

Positive behavioral interventions and supports (PBIS) is a schoolwide strategy that focuses on teaching and encouraging positive behaviors for all students.[33] It brings many of the practices developed in the RtI world to the tasks of behavior management in schools. When NCLB brought about a new data-rich era for school leaders to use information to track and manage school processes, RtI used this new capacity of new school data systems and new forms of assessment to provide learning support services for students. PBIS seeks to use these same resources as RtI to establish a schoolwide culture of behavioral standards and supports.

PBIS adapts several key features of RtI to provide behavioral supports for students. In PBIS, teachers, leaders, psychologists, parents, and staff members meet to discuss data on student behavior, determine school expectations, and celebrate when students meet behavioral goals.[34]

PBIS has three tiers of support for students:

- *Tier 1*, or universal support, invites educators to define and teach behavioral expectations for all students and to develop common practices to reward desired behaviors. Data on all students are collected and discussed by educators to identify students in need of additional support.

- In *tier 2*, students who have problems with appropriate behavior check in with designated adults to plan their days. These students typically carry a "point card" they share with teachers to track behavioral goals.

- *Tier 3* is for students who have difficulty with the intermittent check-ins and require a more intensive behavioral plan.[35]

Often the shared structures of RtI and PBIS knit support staff together in a common framework to address learning and disciplinary issues. As with RtI, studying the effects of PBIS is a lively topic for research. Some researchers found that successful implementation of PBIS can result in a reduction of the number of students referred out of the classroom for disciplinary reasons, fewer suspensions from school, and even improved learning outcomes.[36] However, the variation in how PBIS is adapted to local contexts makes high-quality research difficult to conduct.

A central critique is that PBIS overlooks the role of culture in student learning and behavior. By framing student behavioral issues in terms of shared goals and data about referrals and violations, the kinds of peer relations and cultural contexts that make behavioral goals meaningful for young people can be stripped from the context. Aydin Bal, Kathleen King Thorius, and Elizabeth Kozleski argue that a culturally responsive form of PBIS (CRPBIS) would identify and build on these practices as resources to shape student behavior.[37] The PBIS model of adopting schoolwide behavioral standards can tend to reward students already familiar with the cultural assumptions built into behavioral expectations, which can unintentionally penalize students from families who do not come to school familiar with the practices of the dominant culture. A CRPBIS model works with students and families to bridge the cultures of home and school into negotiated standards and a menu of consequences that shape the context for positive behavioral interventions and supports.

Restorative Justice

Restorative justice is an approach toward establishing a safe and effective learning environment that empowers student peer groups to judge the consequences of their actions. The idea of restorative justice is rooted in criminal justice discussions about the role that acknowledgment and reparation by offenders can play in remediating the harm done to victims. A restorative justice model invites the offender to make amends to victims in accordance with terms established by the peer community.[38] This path allows members of a school community to own their behavioral standards and to go beyond exclusion by teaching appropriate behavior through acts of healing.[39]

The process of remediation in restorative justice is typically framed as a deliberative process where the victims and the violators have a chance to tell their stories and a peer group assesses the evidence and prescribes a course of action:[40]

- *Circles.* One approach toward building restorative justice practice is the peacemaking circle, a structure that allows people to talk about and resolve conflict. The circle has a leader, or keeper, who invites the violators and the victims to share their stories about what happened. Other circle members listen and assess what is being shared, then discuss the consequences for the actors involved. In schools, circle members are mainly students, and a condition of the successful interaction of the circle is that the violators agree to be bound by the judgment of the circle members.

- *Mediation and conferencing.* Mediation and conferencing are conducted in conflicts between two (or more) students. A trained mediator facilitates interaction with the students in conflict and invites students and educators to listen and participate in the resolution process. In peer mediation, students are trained to serve as the conflict mediators. Students apprentice by observing and gradually becoming more involved in assisting in mediation. Using peer mediation as a method to address minor issues can prevent escalation and also provides student mediators with valuable interpersonal skills.

- *Youth courts.* Student volunteers serve on youth courts as a jury for peer offenses. Typically an educator is the moderator for the court, but the juries hear cases and determine agreements for the violators to repair damage to the community. Jury members should represent the student body and should also include students who have appeared before the jury so that all members of the community can participate in both sides of the experience.

These kinds of structures, when successfully implemented, can reduce the number of situations that escalate into criminal justice cases while building strong peer communities that come to define and own standards for appropriate interaction.

Restorative justice is particularly important for public education. Students come to school to develop social as well as academic skills. Restorative justice builds on the PBIS insight that schools need to teach (as well as enforce) behavioral expectations and adds practices that seek to turn violations of expected behaviors into opportunities for learning and healing. Thalia Gonzalez explains:

> The underlying assumption of restorative justice is that students who commit delinquent or offensive acts are breaching the social contract of between them and the school community. That social contract cannot be restored if the breaching party is absent—that is, if the school's first and most frequent response is to ban the offender from the community. . . . Restorative practices emphasize the importance of relationships.[41]

Restorative justice programs assume that the behavioral environment is built by students and educators together. Gonzalez describes the result of this co-construction as a social contract that binds community members together in terms of mutual agreement. Unlike classical social contract theory in which violators are cast out of society, restorative justice requires members to bring violators back into the society to make amends. Restorative justice invites students to determine the consequences for minor violations of the school code. This allows the school to avoid the escalating consequences that ultimately result in exclusion of students from the community. Educators in restorative justice programs look for opportunities to create relational trust by inviting students to resolve problems with one another through conversation and interaction.

This process of building relational trust through restorative justice is a longer-term commitment to engaging students in creating the cultural conditions to own the behavioral standards for the school. Gonzalez concluded that schools should develop a four- to six-year plan for whole-school implementation of a restorative justice program. Just as with the processes for changing faculty culture around relational trust discussed in Chapter 5, the practices of restorative justice depend on students: as community members, they must make good on promises of support and requests for help.

School leaders pressed to make effective changes to acute crises can be tempted by the clear definition and obvious promise of zero-tolerance policies to create safe learning environments. However, as we have seen throughout this book, schools are irreducibly social places, and technical solutions, however tempting they seem, focus on data and structure rather than the kinds of interaction that result in relational trust; they rarely change culture. CRPBIS and restorative justice models describe a road for school leaders to build resilient communities among students that reflect the same values as the professional communities that educators develop to improve teaching and learning.

NOTES

1. Weingarten, R. (2015).
2. Losen, D. J., Hodson, C. L., Keith, I. I., Michael, A., Morrison, K., & Belway, S. (2015).
3. Skiba, R. J., Peterson, R. L., & Williams, T. (1997).
4. Kane, T. J., Taylor, E. S., Tyler, J. H., & Wooten, A. L. (2011).
5. Sebastian, J., & Allensworth, E. (2012).
6. DeAngelis, K. J., & Presley, J. B. (2011).
7. Much in the next three paragraphs is drawn from the excellent overview of the recent history of school disciplinary policies by Kang-Brown, J., Trone, J., Fratello, J., & Daftary-Kapur, T. (2013, December).
8. Butts, J. A., & Travis, J. (2002).
9. See Kang-Brown et al. (2013, pp. 1–2). For a discussion of the impact of the broken windows theory on urban school design, see Livermore, C. (2008).
10. Kang-Brown et al. (2013).
11. U.S. Department of Justice. (2014).
12. Kang-Brown et al. (2013).
13. Fabelo, T., Thompson, M. D., Plotkin, M., Carmichael, D., Marchbanks III, M. P., & Booth, E. A. (2011).
14. Los Angeles Unified School Board Resolution. (2013, May 14); Watanabe, T. (2013, May 12).
15. Robers, S., Kemp, J., & Truman, J. (2013).
16. Irby, D. J. (2013).
17. Kang-Brown et al. (2013, p. 4).
18. Hoffmann, J. P., Erickson, L. D., & Spence, K. R. (2013).
19. Lewis, A. E., & Diamond, J. B. (2015).

20. Irby, D. J. (2014, p. 513).

21. Irby. (2014, p. 514).

22. Mehan, H., Mercer, J., & Rueda, R. (2002).

23. National Center for Education Statistics. (2015).

24. National Center for Education Statistics. (2015).

25. Gresham, F. M. (2007, p. 16).

26. Rebora, A. (2010, April 12).

27. Shah, N. (2011, August 19).

28. For a review of this work, see Gersten, R., Compton, D., Connor, C. M., Dimino, J., Santoro, L., Linan-Thompson, S., & Tilly, W. D. (2008).

29. Balu, R., Zhu, P., Doolittle, F., Schiller, E., Jenkins, J., & Gersten, R. (2015).

30. For discussions about the role of standardization and narrowing the curriculum, see Crocco, M. S., & Costigan, A. T. (2007); also see Kamenetz, A. (2015).

31. See, for example, Gee, J. P. (2007).

32. Artiles, A. J., Bal, A., & King Thorius, K. A. (2010).

33. For more information, see PBIS.org. For a discussion of the research that supports PBIS strategies, see Sugai, G., & Horner, R. (2006).

34. Some schools post videos of the PBIS schoolwide celebrations as a way to share student progress publicly. See, for example, https://www.youtube.com/ user/MPSPBIS.

35. For more detail, see Losen et al. (2015, pp. 208ff).

36. See, for example, Bradshaw, C. P., Mitchell, M. M., & Leaf, P. J. (2010).

37. Bal, A., King-Thorius, K. A., & Kozleski, E. (2012).

38. Zehr, H. (1997).

39. McCluskey, G., Lloyd, G., Kane, J., Riddell, S., Stead, J., & Weedon, E. (2008).

40. The following examples are taken from Ashley, J., & Burke, K. (2010).

41. Gonzalez, T. (2015).

Mapping Leadership Practice

| 1 | Focus on Learning | 2 | Monitoring Teaching & Learning | 3 | Professional Community | 4 | Acquiring & Allocating Resources | 5 | Safe & Effective Environment |

N MIDSUMMER, PRINCIPAL TRINA MEADOWS, WHOM WE MET IN THE Prologue, attended a statewide meeting of education leaders. She learned about the latest programs in response to intervention (RtI), community engagement, and formative assessment. In one session, she was intrigued to hear about the CALL survey as a process to map leadership practices that related to improved student learning. Unlike some of the other products, CALL promised to provide feedback on the local work that educators were doing to monitor and improve instruction and develop a safe learning environment. She spoke with several of her colleagues about CALL and decided to share the survey with her leadership team at Truman.

The leadership team agreed that CALL would help to provide feedback on the messy areas of practice that many of the outcome-oriented assessments and tools glossed over. They also thought that CALL could help Truman define a baseline of practices against which the community could measure progress in domains such as developing a professional community and services for students who struggle. Meadows and her team got district approval to use CALL at the back-to-school teacher meetings in the fall.

The CALL survey process went smoothly. Before taking the survey, teachers and staff logged in to the leadershipforlearning.org site, and jumped right into the 30-minute survey. The initial reactions from teachers on the survey were interesting to the Truman leadership team. Teachers spoke of reflecting on the different levels of the leadership work involved in improving practices and how the survey provided a chance to think about their everyday work. Taking the CALL survey seemed to have had a positive impact on how educators thought and talked about their work.[1]

Truman leaders had feedback on all of the educators' responses right after the last educator finished. Meadows brought her team together shortly after the survey closed to review the results.[2] CALL provides a variety of reports to help educators digest the results of the survey. The first report that Meadows shared with her team was the CALL Top 10, which reported the items from across the survey with the highest scores (Table 8.1).

The top of the list encouraged the leadership team. Truman's efforts to build a learning plan that was shared across all educators was a key priority of the leadership team, and they hoped that the school community would see this commitment in daily practice. Subdomain 1.3 proved the highest-rated item on

Table 8.1 Truman Top 10 Subdomains of Practice

CALL SUBDOMAIN	SCORE
1.3: Collaborative design of integrated learning plan	3.9
3.3: Socially distributed leadership	3.7
1.2: Recognition of formal leaders as instructional leaders	3.7
3.1: Collaborative schoolwide focus on problems of teaching and learning	3.5
4.3: School resources focus on student learning	3.4
2.2: Summative evaluation of student learning	3.4
5.2: Clean and safe learning environment	3.2
4.2: Structuring and maintaining time	3.2
1.1: Maintaining a schoolwide focus on learning	3.1
5.1: Clear, consistent, and enforced expectations for student behavior	3.1

the survey, and 1.1, maintaining a schoolwide focus on learning, made it into the top 10 of practices. Collaborative schoolwide focus on problems of teaching and learning (3.1) and socially distributed leadership (3.3) also had a high rank, indicating to the team that efforts to build relational trust through design were recognized within the school. The leadership team was also pleased to see that the school efforts to establish a safe and effective learning environment (Domain 5) were reflected in the survey findings. Subdomains 5.1 (clear, consistent, and enforced expectations for student behavior) and 5.2 (clean and safe learning environment) all made it into the top 10.

The Truman leaders were surprised to see 2.2 (summative evaluation of student learning) in the top 10 practices. For years teachers and families had struggled with state tests for ninth and tenth graders and the ACT for eleventh graders as required measures of student learning. This score meant that educators around the school now recognized these tests as part of monitoring teaching and learning.

Truman leaders saw that some of the key efforts they had coordinated in recent years were confirmed by the CALL survey. Efforts to participate in staff learning opportunities paid off in the high ranking for subdomain 1.2, and Meadows's early efforts to rein in the multiple narratives alive in the school to zero in on student learning (subdomain 1.1) also proved to be a top 10 practice. Seeing some of their efforts reflected in the CALL survey made Meadows and her team relieved that the hard work and dedication of recent years was paying off in community acknowledgment of key initiatives.

But with reflection, the leadership team began to question these results. The team anxiously dove into the Bottom 10 report (Table 8.2). As they expected, subdomain 3.4, coaching and mentoring, was not rated highly within the school, mainly because the Truman instructional coaching initiative was brand new and limited to supporting only new and struggling teachers. Truman leaders reasoned that the majority of the teachers did not know about coaching and were not in a good position to say much about it. Similarly, the school staff continued to work on efforts to bring parents into school events as part of the community outreach initiative, which was just getting off the ground. It would be good, thought Meadows, to get feedback on subdomains 3.4 and 4.5 after the current initiatives were in play for a while.

More disturbing to the Truman leadership team were the low ratings on services for students who struggled (subdomains 5.3 and 1.4), formative assessment (subdomains 2.1 and 2.3), and professional learning (subdomain 3.2). Each of these issues sparked a long discussion about the relation of leadership initiatives to school practices. In the first discussion on formative assessment, the CALL survey allowed the staff to break down the scores by department. The Truman team observed that the math department teachers who organized their meetings around student data and classroom practice gave a higher score to formative assessment of teaching (2.3) than educators in other departments. This difference suggested that the leadership team should follow up with the math educators to better understand their efforts and share their practices with other departments.

Table 8.2 Truman Bottom 10 Subdomains of Practice

SUBDOMAIN	SCORE
3.4: Coaching and mentoring	1.7
4.5: Coordinating and supervising relations with families and external communities	2.0
2.3: Formative evaluation of teaching	2.1
5.3: Support services for students who traditionally struggle	2.3
1.4: Providing appropriate services for students who traditionally struggle	2.3
2.1: Formative evaluation of student learning	2.6
3.2: Professional learning	2.7
4.1: Personnel practices	2.8
2.4: Summative evaluation of teaching	2.8
4.4: Integrating external expertise into the school instructional program	3.0

The low scores for providing services for students who struggled led to a soul-searching conversation about what to do next in the school. The pioneering work of Meadows and some of the teachers to develop the study skills program and the restorative justice programs did not seem to budge the perception among educators that students of color and English language learners, in particular, were being disproportionately identified for behavioral problems and learning disabilities. The low ratings for subdomains 5.3 and 1.4 confirmed the student outcomes and engagement data reviewed by the leadership team and led the Truman educators to review the specific practices described in these subdomains as a pathway for planning action in the coming year.

The conversation then shifted to patterns that emerged in the scores. First, there was a seemingly persistent gap between leaders' and educators' perceptions of practices. Leaders seemed to disagree with teachers and staff in the rating of most domains and typically rated leadership practices higher than the teachers in their schools did.[3] The disparity in ratings may lie in the perception that establishing the conditions for improving teaching and learning is experienced as work for leaders but as part of the everyday context of schooling for educators. Leaders may be more likely than teachers or other staff to experience or be aware of leadership practices taking place in certain pockets within the school. They may believe that leadership practices observed in individual classrooms or departments are taking place in other classrooms and departments at the same pace. They may believe that best practices discussed in schoolwide meetings are being carried out with fidelity throughout the school. From their big picture perspective, the school appears to be addressing or carrying out higher levels of leadership than the teachers are experiencing.

Then the Truman team turned these insights around and wondered whether the teacher perceptions were correct and that they had overstated their own leadership estimates of practices. Leaders may believe that they are including teacher voices in decision making because representative teachers are at the table. But the teachers who are not at the table may not feel informed or empowered in the process. Across the survey, the only area that Truman teachers rated school practices higher than leaders was in providing appropriate services for students who traditionally struggle. The team felt that this difference might reflect the principal's broader understanding of the persistent problems of equitable programs from the perspective of schoolwide data, while specific teachers might base their judgments on successful interactions with individual students and families. Thinking about Domain 1, Focus on Learning, led the team to discuss how telling the story of leadership efforts more consistently and through coordinated action might help to align the perceptions of leaders and educators on the prevalence of schoolwide practice.[4]

After the meeting, Meadows reflected back on her thoughts about the gaps in the Truman information ecology—gaps that had prevented her from seeing the connections between intentions and outcomes. CALL filled this gap. CALL data mapped the routes from the existing routines of daily practice to instructional initiatives designed to shape new routines. CALL items carefully described gradations in the quality and frequency of practices, then invited the entire school community to give feedback on research-based practices that matter. Thanks to the CALL data, the Truman community now had a good understanding of the state-of-the-school practices of leadership for learning. The next steps were to use CALL data to refine new initiatives to improve teaching and learning across the school.

MAPPING LEADERSHIP PRACTICE

The purpose of this book is to provide a map of K–12 school leadership in 21st-century schools. Our schools are shaped by long-standing public expectations to bridge the gap between the reality of inequality to equal opportunities for all children and families to succeed. In recent years, the demand to address high-stakes accountability, new data technologies, and a widening gap between rich and poor has placed school leaders and educators in a difficult position to satisfy public expectations. Yet in many ways, the tools available to school leaders have never been more generative. Educators have access to a wide range of information and instructional resources and can participate in richer and more wide-ranging professional networks within and across schools. School leaders can get lost in this wealth of expectations, demands, and tools. CALL provides a map to guide a path toward establishing the conditions that improve learning for all students.

CALL unites the research on effective school leadership practices and the perspectives of expert educator communities through a distributed leadership framework. As we discussed in Chapter 2, distributed leadership considers how the work of building capacity is stretched across many people in the school. The principal, to be sure, remains a pivotal leader in the school, but the work of living the story of the school mission, setting up information networks, coordinating professional learning, acquiring and allocating resources, and building a safe learning environment for all students is clearly shared by many educators. Like the navigator in a navy ship, the principal must be aware and must coordinate the work, but without a crew to co-construct the key tasks, the school cannot move intentionally toward its goals.

CALL defines leadership as establishing the conditions for improving teaching and learning. These conditions are the essential features of school improvement. Organized into five domains of practice, the work of leadership is specified in terms of specific tasks that constitute effective leadership practice. As we discussed in Chapters 3 to 7, these are the CALL domains:

- Domain 1: *Focus on Learning* recognizes the diversity of aims in every school community and requires leaders to tell a story, through words and deeds, that links each major initiative to student learning. Through their stories and actions, leaders create a coherent picture of reform and become known throughout the school community as instructional leaders who have the knowledge and experience needed to improve practice.

- Domain 2: *Monitoring Teaching and Learning* requires leaders to build an information ecology from the information sources necessary to improve the process and measure the outcomes of teaching and learning. A successful information ecology not only collects and stores information, but also describes the social practices of reflection and renewed action needed to turn information into improved practice.

- Domain 3: *Building Professional Community* is at the heart of leadership for learning. Professional community is the collected social and intellectual capital within the school needed for engaging in improvement. The core ingredient in professional community is relational trust, which is built through the collaborative design of initiatives grounded in the practice of community members. A successful professional community is socially distributed leadership in action.

- Domain 4: *Acquiring and Allocating Resources* defines how school leaders gather and manage the human and material capital needed to guide school improvement. At a basic level, leaders need to manage the entry (and exit) of educators into the school, bring in money, and organize time for effective practices; at a distributed level, leaders invite participation in relevant professional networks outside the school. The community is both the audience for the school community and the vital partner for improving practice and must be integrated into the everyday work of teaching and learning.

- Domain 5: *Establishing a Safe and Effective Learning Environment* challenges leaders to create an effective balance between high standards for student conduct and disproportionately punishing groups of students for noncompliance. Public design and data-driven review of behavioral expectations and learning spaces are key aspects of Domain 5, as is careful attention to restorative feedback and culturally relevant initiatives for learners to live safe learning spaces on their own terms.

These domains, we suggest, constitute the core practices of effective school leadership. The specification of these domains into practices helps to create a shared vocabulary among educators about the practices that connect the conditions with the outcomes of teaching and learning. This is not to suggest that these domains are in any way exhaustive descriptions of leadership practices. A map is not a terrain. Maps narrow the rich information of a terrain to make a complex space navigable. Building a map always involves the trade-off of information loss with directional gain. We hope that the CALL domains provide a successful trade-off to guide practice. In more recent conversations with educators engaged in, for example, personalized learning or community school reforms, the CALL domains of focus, monitoring, professional community, resources, and learning environments continue to provide helpful guides for the kinds of practices that matter, even if the specific tasks change with the demands of a given reform.

A good map does more than reduce the information in the terrain. It also provides directions toward desired destinations. Seen in this light, the sequencing of the CALL domains supports different perspectives on supporting pathways toward the goals of leadership work in schools. Traditional instructional leadership, for example, focuses on the work of Domains 1, 2, and 3 (Figure 8.1) and takes Domains 4 and 5 for granted as the conditions for engaging in the more advanced work of leadership for learning.

In our early work with refining the items in CALL, we encountered a clear difference in the perspectives of practitioners and researchers about these conditions. Educators noted that researchers could afford to overlook the necessity of Domains 4 and 5 to focus directly on the practices that led directly to instructional improvement. Actual work in schools, though, made it obvious that without adequate resources and a safe learning environment, no advances would ever be made on improving teaching and learning.

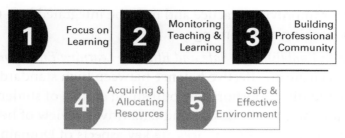

Figure 8.1 Instructional Leadership CALL Map

Our educator partners led us to appreciate what we came to call a Maslovian model of organizing the CALL domains, where leaders must work to establish the basic needs of a school community (Domains 4 and 5) to support the instructional leadership work of Domains 1 to 3 (Figure 8.2).[5] In this view, the ability to address "higher-order" goals, such as the development of an information ecology or engaging in socially distributed leadership, first requires the establishment of order in the school community. Students must pay attention to and master the basic rules of interaction (and basic academic skills) before participating in the design of their own learning paths. Teachers must be active in the hallways monitoring behavior, and teaching practice must address basic information needs (clearly posting lesson objectives in classrooms) before entertaining more ambitious, constructivist behavior and learning goals. Leaders who run a tight ship from a Maslovian perspective that makes teachers and students feel safe to be in a clean, orderly place have satisfied the requirement for the school community to walk before it can run.

The argument between Maslovians and the instructional leaders comes down to the focus of the work. From the instructional leadership perspective, focusing on Domains 4 and 5 will never lead beyond acquiring resources and building safe

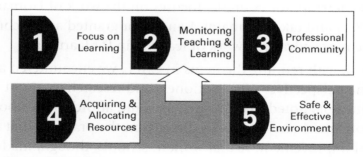

Figure 8.2 Maslovian CALL Map

learning environments. According to the instructional leadership perspective, the Maslovians will have well-resourced, orderly schools with no capacity to improve learning. The Maslovians counter with the practical insight that without safety and resources, there is no risk taking, and without risk, there is no instructional innovation.

The CALL theory of action suggests a resolution to the opposition between these two perspectives grounded in design for relational trust. The CALL approach to mapping leadership is focused on Domain 3, the development of professional community among educators. Educators are directly responsible for working with students every day. Their knowledge, skills, and interactions have the greatest effect on student outcomes. Supporting their capacity to learn from experience is thus a primary condition for improving teaching and learning.

In Chapter 5, we proposed professional community as the heart of the school capacity to improve instruction. Professional community, we explained, results from relational trust built through the collaborative design of initiatives to support classroom practices. A culture rich in relational trust has the flexibility to adapt to emergent challenges of shifting community demographics, new learning standards and technologies, and changes in leadership. The CALL relational trust map places Domain 3, professional community, at the center of the map (Figure 8.3). If professional community is the heart of the school capacity for improvement, then each of the CALL domains both supports and results from the practices of Domain 3:

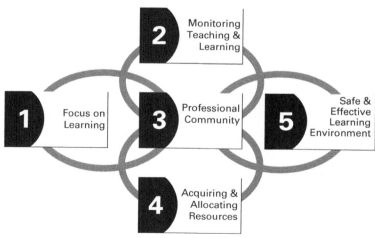

Figure 8.3 CALL Theory of Action Map

- *Domain 1: Focus on Learning.* The lived story of Focus on Learning shapes the direction of initial efforts to define the design activities that form the relational trust of professional community and establishes the credibility of formal leaders to guide the teaching and learning process. As professional community develops, the story of the school mission is refined and can begin to address some of the chronic areas of school improvement. For example, an initial school goal of "getting control over instructional time" can lead educators to move toward "giving students control over their instructional time." The Maslovian development metaphor is seen as an interactive process where the focus on learning becomes more refined as the capacity to envision and address problems grows.

- *Domain 2: Monitoring Teaching and Learning.* Leaders need high-quality information to guide the process and measure the outcomes of teaching and learning. Building an information ecology begins with implementing tools given to the school by state and district policies. Making information useful requires leaders to challenge cultures of loose coupling in order to make classrooms open to formative data collection and consultation for both teachers and students. In an effective school, the practices of monitoring teaching and learning are collaboratively designed to build a shared sense of mission, then used to generate information to inform internal and external communities about the quality of teaching and learning practices.

- *Domain 4: Acquiring and Allocating Resources.* Building professional community calls on human, information, and material resources. In the initial state of Domain 4 practices, leaders establish networks to bring resources into the school community and support new and struggling educators to succeed. Over time, these networks blossom into professional networks that involve educators from across the school in bringing valued resources into the school and participate in induction, mentoring, and coaching initiatives to support one another. As with the other domains, the practices of acquiring and allocating resources first establish the conditions for improving teaching and learning and then are used to sustain continuous improvement of professional growth.

- *Domain 5: Establishing a Safe and Effective Learning Environment.* Learning is a risky process. It requires a safe space where learners—whether teachers or students—can express typically faulty conceptions in order to move toward better knowledge and skills. Relational trust suggests that schools lacking safe spaces need to engage in collaborative design around shared behavioral policies and practices. When new practices get a foothold, the relational trust established among educators, students, and families gives a foundation for taking risks in order to improve. The trust built by behavioral initiatives, however, will not translate into instructional knowledge and skills without leaders who can create opportunities that convert one form of relational trust into another. Domain 5 practices describe a basic need for all school communities that must serve as a resource for further capacity development.

The CALL leadership practice shows the routes toward school improvement and describes the practices necessary to maintain and build capacity. It is grounded not in a deficit model of replacing local capital with imported knowledge and skills or new staff, but in strategies through which the school community creates the capacity it needs to face emerging challenges through collaborative design. It describes practices for schools that need to transform toxic into generative cultures, and it shows leaders who have built capacity for improvement how to take their schools to the next level.

USING THE CALL MAP

Meadows and the Truman leadership team illustrate the primary use of CALL. The Truman school community took the survey and used the ideas built into the domains and items to target key tasks for developing a school improvement plan. The unique perspective that CALL provides on improvement practices has other uses as well.

Baseline Data for Strategic Planning

Several of our districts use CALL as an information source for strategic planning. Schools and districts need baseline data when planning for improvement. Typically leaders bring together stakeholders to set priorities, specify resources, and determine outcome measures in order to build shared agreement about process and goals. CALL can provide data about the practices necessary to bring about change in the school. CALL domains and items can serve as baseline data to measure the progress of the change, or the domains themselves (such as building professional community or a safe learning environment) can become goals for strategic planning. When complemented by other outcome measures, CALL can give stakeholders a sense of ongoing progress toward goals

New Leadership Induction

One of the professional organizations in a large urban district provides CALL as a service to ease the transition of new leaders into schools. New leaders typically lack experience of the routines and culture of their new school. CALL can give them a big picture perspective of school capacity. It can describe community strengths and areas for improvement, and because the CALL reports can describe individual departments or units, new leaders can get a good sense of where the most work is needed. Discrepancies between the scores of educators and positional leaders can indicate the degree to which a coherent story of improvement is shared across the school. These kinds of data can accelerate the process for a new leader to engage with the existing school culture in sparking change.

Research Study Measures of Leadership and School Culture

The CALL team has had success working with research groups interested in measuring the impact of interventions. Researchers often have little sense of the history and culture of their school partners. Assessing the impact of an intervention means ruling out contextual factors that can obscure the causes of change. Inviting the schools to take the CALL survey gives a rich sense of the prevalent practices in the school. This sense of the context of practice helps researchers to develop more sophisticated analyses of the impact of interventions.

Leadership Preparation Programs

CALL is a framework to organize the essential practices of school leadership. These essential practices can serve as the program for school leadership preparation as well as an outcome measure to ensure quality leadership learning. Our K–12 Leadership Preparation Program at the University of Wisconsin-Madison uses CALL as a template to organize the course work necessary for professional certification. The CALL domains then serve as the categories of a portfolio-based assessment that measures the quality of learning attained by students in the program.

We have experience in supporting schools and researchers in each of these uses of CALL. Access to these kinds of rich, collective descriptions of leadership practice is a handy resource for guiding school improvement at any level.

CHARTING THE COURSE TO IMPROVED TEACHING AND LEARNING

Over time, the challenges that schools face will continue to change. New information technologies, for example, will reshape the role that students play in directing their own learning. Growing economic disparities will push schools that already serve as community lighthouses into a more prominent role for families to access health care, immigrant services, and counseling supports. Charter polices will encourage districts to experiment with a wider variety of schools, within existing schools and in their own spaces, specializing in arts and technical programs. The CALL map cannot predict the future of public schools (no map is *that* good!). However, as long as schools are organized around educator interaction with students, school leaders will need to establish the conditions for maintaining and improving learning. Leaders now and in the future will need to focus on learning and build information ecologies, professional communities, resource networks, and safe learning environments. The individual practices may change in CALL, but the research-driven domains it describes will always have value for improving teaching and learning.

In *Sensemaking and Organizations*, Karl Weick famously stated, "When you are lost, any old map will do."[6] He related a story about an army unit lost in the Alps during a blizzard. The unit was feared lost, then turned up two days later. One soldier had found a map in his pocket, which calmed his colleagues and gave them the courage to find their way out of the mountains. It turned out that the map was of the Pyrenees, not the Alps. Weick explains that the simple availability of a map can mobilize, coordinate action, and provide a focus for collective action. School leaders today are in a much better position than Weick's lost soldiers.

Contemporary leaders can draw on rich resources of scholarship and practice to direct action in their schools. Most schools have made tremendous investments in building the capacity of each of the CALL domains. Unlike Weick's soldiers, educators in K–12 schools are awash in information about current and best practices. CALL provides a map to coordinate action in an information-rich world in schools with many competing goals. It brings these ideas together to provide a comprehensive map to guide school improvement. While any old map might do, CALL is not any old map. It is the map that school leaders need to describe the world of school improvement and chart a course toward improving teaching and learning for all.

NOTES

1. Carolyn Kelley and Seann Dikkers (2016) found CALL users reported that CALL feedback provided transparency in communicating a clear theory of action for planning and fostered formal and informal conversations around school improvement.
2. The CALL results reported here are a composite of several high schools of similar size and demographics to the fictional Truman community.
3. The gap between leader and teacher ratings is also confirmed on other schoolwide assessments of leadership practice. See, for example, Goff, P. T., Goldring, E., & Bickman, L. (2014).
4. A. Bowers, M. Blitz, M. Modest, J. Salisbury, and R. Halverson (2017) studied patterns in CALL results to describe three groups of schools: (1) schools with low leader and teacher ratings, (2) schools with high leader and teacher ratings, and (3) schools with high leader and low teacher ratings. They found that new leaders often ended up in group 1, and that group 2 included veteran leaders and educators who had worked together to align perceptions of leaders and educators on leadership practices. Schools in group 3, they recommend, should work on practices to align perceptions in order to form a coherent school community with a common recognition of practices.
5. Abraham Maslow's groundbreaking concept of a hierarchy of needs has been popularized to describe any sequential developmental process. Maslow's original (1954) version described deficiency needs, such as appetite and physical safety, that, if not met, make it difficult for people to attain higher self-actualization goals. Maslow's hierarchy has been widely criticized by subsequent generations of developmental psychology research, but it retains its power as a metaphor to describe the conditions that must be met to reach advanced goals. For more detail, see Maslow, A. (1954), and Wahba, M. A., & Bridwell, L. G. (1976).
6. Weick, K. (1999).

APPENDIX A

CALL Research Publications

Blitz, M. (2012). *A case study comparison of school leadership practice against the Comprehensive Assessment of Leadership for Learning (CALL) Pilot Results* (WCER Working Paper No. 2012–5). Retrieved from http://www.wcer.wisc.edu/publications/workingPapers/papers.php

Blitz, M. H., & Modeste, M. (2015). The differences across distributed leadership practices by school position according to the Comprehensive Assessment of Leadership for Learning (CALL). *Leadership and Policy in Schools, 14*(3), 341–379.

Blitz, M., Salisbury, J., & Kelley, C. (2014). The role of cognitive validity testing in the development of CALL, the Comprehensive Assessment of Leadership for Learning. *Journal of Educational Administration, 52*(3), 358–378.

Bowers, A. J., Blitz, M., Modest, M., Salisbury, J., & Halverson, R. (2017). How leaders agree with teachers in schools on measures of leadership practice: A two-level latent class analysis of the Comprehensive Assessment of Leadership for Learning. *Teachers College Record, 119*(1), 1–38.

Goff, P., Salisbury, J., & Blitz, M. (2015, October). *Comparing CALL and VAL-ED: An illustrative application of a decision matrix for selecting among leadership feedback instruments* (WCER Working Paper No. 2015-5). Retrieved from http://wcer-web.ad.education.wisc.edu/docs/working-papers/Working_Paper_No_2015_05.pdf

Halverson, R., Kelley, C., & Shaw, J. (2014). A CALL for improved school leadership. *Phi Delta Kappan, 95*(6), 57–60.

Kelley, C., & Dikkers, S. (2016). Framing feedback for school improvement around distributed leadership. *Educational Administration Quarterly, 52*(3), 392–422.

Kelley, Carolyn, & Halverson, Richard. (2012). "The Comprehensive Assessment of Leadership for Learning: A Next Generation Formative Evaluation and Feedback System." *Journal of Applied Research on Children: Informing Policy for Children at Risk 3*(2), art. 4. Retrieved from http://digitalcommons.library.tmc.edu/childrenatrisk/vol3/iss2/4

Kelley, C., & Salisbury, J. (2013). Defining and activating the role of department chair as instructional leader. *Journal of School Leadership, 23*(2), 287–323.

Modeste, M., & Kelley, C. (2016). Distributed leadership and the comprehensive assessment of leadership for learning. In H. Bjerg & N. Vaaben (Eds.), *Leading for learning.* Copenhagen, Denmark: Samfunds Litteratur.

CALL Research Publications

[reversed/mirrored text — bibliography entries not legibly reproducible]

APPENDIX B

Observations about Some Differences in CALL Results between Secondary and Elementary Schools

An examination of the CALL data suggests differences in the ways elementary and secondary educators rate school leadership practices. Elementary schools tend to rate higher across the board in leadership practices than their secondary school peers do. This appendix presents finding of the differences between elementary and secondary schools, and between school leader and teacher perceptions using our pilot data set. We present these analyses of trends from our pilot work that have persisted throughout the CALL data. These trends are not surprising, given several characteristics of elementary schools that have been documented in leadership research:

- *Elementary administrators supervise fewer teachers*, which contributes to better communication, better ability to monitor and supervise teachers, greater cohesion in the focus on learning, and greater ability to build coherent academic programs within and across grade levels.
- *Elementary teachers work with fewer students.* Each elementary school teacher might work daily with 25 to 30 students; in secondary schools, each teacher might work with 150 to 250 students each day.

- *Elementary schools strategically leverage special teachers* (such as physical education, health, art, and music) to enable grade-level teachers to meet and collaborate around problems of practice. This is more challenging in secondary schools, where scheduling is driven by student needs and teachers may be the only ones teaching a particular subject (making collaboration less fruitful).
- *School safety issues and student behavior management are easier in elementary schools.* Smaller school size and younger children enable the development of teacher-student relationships that can overcome some behavioral challenges.

Tables B.1 and B.2 show teacher ratings of distributed leadership practices in elementary schools and in middle and high schools, based on the CALL pilot survey data. The first thing you might note is that the highest-rated leadership practice in middle and high schools is rated lower than the lowest-rated leadership practice in elementary schools. In our work with CALL schools, we have come to expect that leadership practices intended to reshape teaching and learning have a more limited scope in secondary schools. Perhaps this is because of the prevalence of other levels of leadership in secondary schools (e.g., department chairs); perhaps it is because of the greater autonomy of practice expected by secondary school teachers.

The next thing to notice is the ranking itself. The highest-rated leadership practices in elementary schools are associated with the influence of accountability

Table B.1 Top Practices in Elementary Schools

	PRACTICE	SCORE
2.2	Summative evaluation of student learning	4.0
1.1	Maintaining a schoolwide focus on learning	3.9
3.2	Professional learning	3.9
2.1	Formative evaluation of student learning	3.9
1.2	Recognition of formal leaders as instructional leaders	3.8
5.1	Clear, consistent, and enforced expectations for student behavior	3.8
2.4	Summative evaluation of teaching	3.7
4.2	Structuring and maintaining time	3.7
1.4	Providing appropriate services for students who traditionally struggle	3.7

Source: Adapted from Modeste and Kelley (2015).

Table B.2 Top Practices in Secondary Schools: Teacher Ratings

	PRACTICE	SCORE
1.4	Providing appropriate services for students who traditionally struggle	2.7
5.1	Clear, consistent, and enforced expectations for student behavior	2.7
2.2	Summative evaluation of student learning	2.7
2.1	Formative evaluation of student learning	2.6
3.2	Professional learning	2.6
5.2	Clean and safe learning environment	2.5
1.2	Recognition of formal leaders as instructional leaders	2.5
1.1	Maintaining a schoolwide focus on learning	2.5
5.3	Support services for students who traditionally struggle	2.5

Source: Adapted from Modeste and Kelly (2015).

policies in schools. Summative evaluation of student learning (2.1), maintaining a schoolwide focus on learning (1.1), professional learning (3.2), and formative evaluation of student learning (2.1) all refer to capacities schools are pressed to develop to meet the demands of test-based accountability policies (We said more about this in Chapter 4.) Elementary schools in particular have focused on examining data from state tests and aligning curriculum to the standards that underlie these tests to ensure that they are teaching students the material that they are expected to know.

The result is a shift in elementary school leadership from letting teachers develop their own pedagogical approaches to making the school responsible for student mastery of the material. It is not enough to cover the material and test students on their ability to do it; teachers need to develop practices that ensure students can demonstrate knowledge on tests. The shift requires analysis and use of student test score data to set goals for instruction, professional development, and analysis of student work to rethink ways of teaching so that students will learn, all reflected in a clear schoolwide focus on student learning.

In contrast, the highest scores in the secondary school responses seem to reflect a pre-test-based accountability-era concern with leaders establishing the noninstructional aspects of schooling. The priority of practices such as providing services for students who struggle and clear and consistent expectations for student behavior point to an expectation that leaders take care of the world outside the classroom while teachers take care of business inside. The contrast between the role of accountability in elementary and secondary schools has yet to be decided: secondary schools may be drawn further into the world of data-driven accountability practices or elementary schools may revert to a time when teachers had the autonomy to guide their own instructional practices.

To create the schoolwide focus, the ratings of 3.9 to 4.0 mean that school leaders set aside frequent, formal opportunities for teachers to discuss student achievement data, student grades, and grading practices. Teachers have developed a common language for discussing instructional practices across grade levels and specialties. Teachers report that professional development activities have improved their teaching, and administrators conduct teaching observations following professional development activities to ensure that teachers are implementing the new approaches correctly in their classrooms.

In secondary schools, we see different leadership practices making the top of the list and much lower ratings on all of the practices. The differences are meaningful. Characteristic of high schools, top-rated practices include providing appropriate services for students who traditionally struggle; clear, consistent, and enforced expectations for student behavior; summative evaluation of student learning; and buffering the teaching environment.

What do these ratings mean? While providing appropriate services for students who traditionally struggle emerged as the top-rated practice, a 2.7 rating means that teachers typically scored their schools between 2 and 3 on the survey items related to this subdomain. A 3 means that students are placed in regular classrooms but the learning goals are set by special education teachers. A 2 means that students are placed in regular classrooms without accommodations for their special learning needs. Higher levels of practice in this subdomain would have regular education and special education teachers working together to develop instructional plans that accommodate the needs of identified and unidentified students.

The second-highest-ranked item, clear, consistent, and enforced expectations for student behavior, provides similar cause for concern. The rating suggests that on average, teachers view student behavior policy as under development or developed but not used. Student behavior is a significant predictor of student success in high school, so the lack of a policy that is consistently enforced is a significant concern.

In addition, the 2.69 rating on summative evaluation of student learning suggests a weak relationship between state tests and student learning goals. In other words, students may or may not be instructed on the material covered in the state tests.

For educators concerned about the quality of teaching and learning in high schools, a quick look at the lowest-rated practices in secondary schools is also cause for concern. All four of these leadership practices represent practices designed to strengthen teaching and learning: coaching and mentoring, summative evaluation of teaching, formative evaluation of teaching, and personnel practices.

Coaching and mentoring ranks low because the resources for coaches and mentors in high schools are so limited that most of the schools indicate they do not have a coaching and mentoring program. This ranks them a 1 on the survey. The two next-to-the-lowest ranked practices are formative and summative evaluation of teaching. Our research on evaluation in high schools suggests that many high school teachers are not regularly observed or evaluated. The rating of 1.8 and 2.0 on these practices means that teachers do not receive formative feedback or the feedback typically includes only generic, positive statements about their teaching. Regarding summative evaluation, teachers are minimally observed and they report that the process does not improve their teaching.

The 1.7 rating of personnel practices indicates that school leaders fail to take into account teacher skills in making teaching assignments, with assignments more typically made based on seniority rather than expertise or skill level. Induction programs for new teachers either do not exist or are not used.

APPENDIX C

Description of the CALL Research and Validation Project

Development of the CALL survey instrument began in 2009 with the support of a four-year grant from the U.S. Department of Education (award R305A090265) to design and validate a survey to provide formative feedback to school leaders on school improvement. To ensure that the survey met what we viewed as four essential design criteria, the process of designing survey items required attention to design issues consistent with the formative nature of the assessment. Specifically, each item was designed to be:

- Aligned with research on effective elementary, middle, and high schools
- Grounded in leadership tasks rather than perceptions about leadership or organizational qualities
- Framed to communicate the underlying theory of action, so that the process of taking the survey would serve as a developmental experience for school leaders and instructional staff
- Consistent with best practices in survey design

Portions of this appendix were drawn from J. Salisbury, E. Camburn, C. Kelley, R. Halverson, P. Goff, S. Kimball, . . . S. Durga. (2013). *The Comprehensive Assessment of Leadership for Learning: Technical report.* Madison: Wisconsin Center for Education Research, University of Wisconsin-Madison.

To ensure that these criteria were met, an initial draft of the survey was developed by the research team based on rubrics created by Richard Halverson in conjunction with the University of Pittsburgh Institute for Learning (IFL). These rubrics were consistent with research conducted by Carolyn Kelley and James Shaw on leadership in schools that had consistently closed achievement gaps and improved overall student learning.[1] We also conducted extensive reviews of research on effective elementary, middle, and high school leadership and on each of the domains of practice to ensure that item development was consistent with the research literature on effective leadership for learning and, more specifically, on the practices represented by specific survey domains, subdomains, and individual items.

Distributed leadership analyses propose that practice is composed of macro- and microtasks.[2] *Macrotasks* refer to general organizational tasks, such as providing adequate resources, planning, and designing professional development, that organize much of the work of school leadership. *Microtasks* articulate these general responsibilities into the day-to-day activities of school leaders. Our survey design work translated microtasks into items that described practices that could be observed by teachers, leaders, and staff in a typical school context.

Our initial focus on middle and high school leadership contexts led us to describe microtasks to reflect the appropriate departmental, grade level, and instructional staff (e.g., special education, counseling, instructional coaches, and mentor) contexts. A major goal of the survey design process was to ground survey items in choice options that reflect actual practices rather than framing responses in terms of perceptions of leadership practice (e.g., "strongly agree" to "strongly disagree" or "not at all" to "to a great extent"). The resulting survey has a relatively high cognitive demand, but the items reflect actual practices in schools, consistent with a clearly specified model of leadership.

Validating CALL

In conducting the validation study for CALL, our research team worked to ensure that the instrument was valid and reliable, as well as meaningful as a formative assessment instrument. To accomplish these goals, we engaged in a series of qualitative and quantitative analyses beginning in spring 2010 and ending in summer 2013. Qualitative analyses included focus groups addressing question content and wording, interviews of pilot participants focusing on survey design and content, and a quality control analysis to ensure that data entered into the survey matched data retrieved from the instrument.

Quantitative analyses included various psychometric analyses and a variance decomposition analysis. The sections that follow provide a detailed description of the individual validation stages for the CALL instrument.

Content Validity

Over two months in spring 2010, a series of focus groups were conducted with two groups of practitioners. The purpose of the focus groups was to obtain practitioner input on survey content and question wording. Each group, one from a middle school and one from a high school, had approximately seven practitioners. Each group met seven times, and in the final meeting, the middle and high schools groups met together.

The first of the seven focus group meetings was used to introduce participants to the goals of the CALL project, highlight expectations for group participants, and review a draft survey. Group members were provided with information about the five domains making up the CALL instrument, the research supporting those domains, the historical context of the tool's development, and the formative feedback nature of the instrument. Once the groups were versed in the background of CALL, they were provided a paper version of the survey to complete and record notes on. Participants were asked to take notes related to their general impression of the survey or to write about other things that piqued their interest. After reading the instrument and taking notes, focus group participants shared their general thoughts of the survey, as well as their general concerns. Their comments were recorded by the research team through field notes and by collecting the copies on which participants had recorded their notes. Generally participant comments during the session were centered on the structure and content of the survey as a whole as opposed to individual items.

Each of the next five sessions was devoted to one of the domains measured on the survey. All five sessions followed the same format. Focus group members were provided an overview of the domain and then given approximately 20 minutes to complete a paper copy of the survey items in that domain. While taking the survey, participants were encouraged to take notes on anything that caught their attention (e.g., question content, missing material, subjective wording, double-barreled questions). Upon completion of the paper survey, the facilitator went through the domain item by item, at which point participants were asked to voice concerns or comments on the given item. During the review of items, the facilitator projected a word document of the survey using an LCD projector. Typically multiple individuals had comments about items, and dialogue would begin about the item in question. During this process, researchers asked clarifying questions and recorded conversations in the form of field notes. Once the group had reached consensus on the question, the facilitator would use track changes to document the edits the focus group had suggested. This process was repeated until all items of interest had been discussed. The final step during these five meetings was to cover items that focus groups felt should be added to the domain in order to accurately capture the practices of a school related to that specific construct.

Following the middle and high school focus group sessions, the CALL research team met to share the results of the respective groups. During these sessions, the team looked at the comments from the two focus groups and worked to make changes to the instrument that aligned with both sets of comments. Typically there was agreement between the high school and middle school groups, but in cases where there was disagreement, the team discussed the difference and applied their professional judgment to revise the instrument to best address both groups' concerns.

The final focus group meeting brought the middle and high school groups together. Participants were provided with an updated version of the survey to complete and take notes on. Following this exercise, the group discussed any lingering concerns over item construction, item content, or missing items. As with previous focus group sessions, the research team recorded participant comments and collected the paper copies of the instrument as another form of data. During the last part of the final focus group, participants were shown screenshots of the online version of the CALL survey and asked for comments or suggestions. As a whole, the focus group was pleased with the online formatting of the instrument and had no major suggestions for improvement.

Following the final practitioner focus group, the research team met to discuss the suggested changes made by participants and come to consensus on possible edits. The result of these focus groups and synthesizing meetings was a version of the instrument ready to be converted into an online tool for pilot schools to take.

In January 2012 CALL contracted with the University of Wisconsin Survey Center (UWSC) to provide feedback on updated survey questions, design a new Web-based CALL instrument, provide data management services for CALL data, and advise the CALL team in the second round of piloting CALL. One of the largest university-based survey centers in the country, the center conducts thousands of telephone, face-to-face, mail, and Web surveys and focus groups annually and achieves consistently high response rates across all survey methodologies. The

UWSC has particularly strong expertise in survey design and question wording under the direction of Nora Cate Schaeffer, a nationally recognized expert in these areas.

UWSC questionnaire experts reviewed the CALL survey and made detailed suggestions for improvements based on current research in the area of survey development. These suggested changes included using common language that all participants will understand, eliminating mouse-over definitions for technical terms in favor of definitions embedded in the stems of questions, adding additional response options to eliminate double-barreled responses, and ensuring that all questions are worded as questions as opposed to statements. In addition, the UWSC recommended the addition of screener questions to allow participants to skip questions that are not relevant to them or their schools.

User Testing

An initial online version of the CALL instrument was piloted in over 70 schools during winter 2011. These pilot schools were broken into two groups: schools that were all located in Mississippi and were solicited to take both CALL and VAL-ED, the 360-degree leadership assessment developed by a research team at Vanderbilt University (see http://www.valed.com). Over 65 schools were in this section of the pilot study. In the second group were six schools from two districts in Wisconsin that were in close geographic proximity to the research team. Schools in this second group were not asked to take the VAL-ED leadership assessment, but were instead asked to participate in exit-style interviews following completion of the CALL instrument. By the end of the initial pilot of CALL, over 1,700 teachers and over 150 school leaders had taken the instrument in two states.

Item Analysis

During summer 2011, the CALL research team conducted a reliability analysis, a Rasch analysis, and a variance decomposition analysis as mechanisms to improve the CALL instrument prior to entering the validation study. These pilot validation studies were completed on the data from the schools in Mississippi and Wisconsin. The goal of these analyses was to make large-grain adjustments to CALL prior to entering the final large-scale validation study.

After changes to the pilot version of CALL were made, our research team began the process of validating the final version of CALL. From spring 2012 through

Table C.1 Cronbach's Alpha Reliability by Subdomain

SUBDOMAIN		CRONBACH'S ALPHA TEACHER	CRONBACH'S ALPHA LEADER	CRONBACH'S ALPHA OTHER	NUMBER OF ITEMS
1.1	Maintaining a schoolwide focus on learning	0.766	0.724	0.751	7
1.2	Recognition of formal leaders as instructional leaders	0.778	0.705	0.765	5
1.3	Collaborative design of integrated learning plan	0.699	0.606	0.681	4
1.4	Providing appropriate services for students who traditionally struggle	0.751	0.741	0.774	9
2.1	Formative evaluation of student learning	0.808	0.831	0.837	9
2.2	Summative evaluation of student learning	0.573	0.619	0.558	5
2.3	Formative evaluation of teaching	0.828	0.707	0.866	8
2.4	Summative evaluation of teaching	0.878	0.816	0.887	9
3.1	Collaborative schoolwide focus on problems of teaching and learning	0.77	0.724	0.817	9
3.2	Professional learning	0.668	0.709	0.738	4
3.3	Socially distributed leadership	0.886	0.836	0.905	12
3.4	Coaching and mentoring	0.829	0.794	0.867	10
4.1	Personnel practices	0.551	0.399	0.587	9
4.2	Structuring and maintaining time	0.662	0.464	0.683	10
4.3	School resources focus on student learning	0.816	0.723	0.832	7

SUBDOMAIN		CRONBACH'S ALPHA TEACHER	CRONBACH'S ALPHA LEADER	CRONBACH'S ALPHA OTHER	NUMBER OF ITEMS
4.4	Integrating external expertise into the school instructional program	0.526	0.44	0.564	4
4.5	Coordinating and supervising relations with families and external communities	0.616	0.55	0.656	6
5.1	Clear, consistent, and enforced expectations for student behavior	0.885	0.882	0.888	21
5.2	Clean and safe learning environments	0.881	0.847	0.87	18
5.3	Support services for students who traditionally struggle	0.788	0.754	0.757	14

spring 2013, 4,567 participants in 129 schools took the CALL survey. Using these data, the CALL research team conducted a final validation analysis of the CALL instrument with a reliability analysis, a Rasch analysis, and a variance decomposition. Results from these analyses included eliminating items that did not align psychometrically with various subdomains and the creation of a scaled scoring system through a Rasch analysis in order to assess the comparability of the scales across items.

For the reliability analysis, we set a threshold of 0.7 as an acceptable reliability statistic for subdomains prior to running our analysis. Subdomains with reliability scores below that threshold underwent scrutiny in future analyses. However, at this point, no items were eliminated; instead, they were noted for future consideration. As we show in Table C.1, 14 of 21, or 66%, subdomains met the reliability threshold for all three user roles: teacher, leader, and support staff. Subdomains of particular interest for the research team were 1.3, 2.2, 4.1, 4.2, and 4.4 because all three user roles had reliability scores below 0.7. In addition, subdomain 3.2 was of interest because the reliability score for teachers was below 0.7, while the other two user roles had a score of above 0.7.

Next, we employed a Rasch analysis to further assess the reliability of subdomains within the CALL instrument. A Rasch analysis identifies misfit items through the production of infit and outfit statistics. Infit statistics demonstrate the degree with which responses for a given item vary from the expected difficulty hierarchy, whereas outfit statistics highlight items that have high numbers of outlier responses. For the purposes of our analysis, we used a cutoff point of 1.2 for both infit and outfit mean square statistics as the point at which items were identified for concern.

As demonstrated in Table C.2, the majority of subdomains within CALL had low numbers of misfit items. In terms of infit statistics, 16 of the 21 subdomains had two or fewer items with infit statistics above 1.2, and 14 of 21 subdomains had

Table C.2 Rasch Item Fit Statistics for Subdomain Scales

SUBDOMAIN	NUMBER OF ITEMS	ITEMS WITH INFIT MEAN SQUARE ABOVE 1.2	ITEMS WITH OUTFIT MEAN SQUARE BELOW 1.2
1.1	8	0	2
1.2	5	1	2
1.3	4	0	0
1.4	15	5	5
2.1	16	1	5
2.2	6	0	1
2.3	14	1	1
2.4	14	2	2
3.1	12	2	1
3.2	5	0	0
3.3	11	2	2
3.4	11	1	1
4.1	7	2	2
4.2	10	2	4
4.3	8	3	3
4.4	4	0	0
4.5	11	3	4
5.1	20	8	7
5.2	20	4	4
5.3	10	2	3

two or fewer items with outfit statistics of above 1.2. Subdomains of particular interest were 1.4, 4.3, 4.5, and 5.2 due to all of them having high numbers of items with infit and outfit statistics greater than 1.2. In addition, subdomains 2.1, 4.2, 5.1, and 5.3 were of modest concern because these subdomains contained more than two items above the threshold for either infit or outfit statistics. As a result of the Rasch analysis, items were eliminated from subdomains; these adjustments are highlighted at the end of this section.

Beyond using the Rasch analysis as a means to ensure that items were appropriately located within subdomains, our research team also used this analysis to scale construct scores for each of the CALL domains and subdomains. Prior to scaling domain and subdomain scores through the Rasch analysis, construct scores were generated as mean scores for the items in a subdomain. While mean scores make intuitive sense, they do not take various nuances into account—issues such as item difficulty and the number of response options for a given item. Using Rasch scores for domains and subdomains provided a score that is more easily compared across the instrument because they place all scales onto a five-point scale.

As with the 2011 pilot analysis, we conducted a variance decomposition analysis to investigate the levels of within school agreement on the CALL subdomain scores. It was our belief that since CALL is designed to provide formative feedback to schools, we should see high levels of within-school agreement on subdomain scores. To accomplish this analysis, we conducted a two-level hierarchical linear model (HLM), which nested teachers within their schools. Results from this analysis are highlighted in Table C.3.

Overall, we found that the CALL subdomains were able to discriminate among schools in a reliable fashion. All 20 CALL subdomains and five domains have a school-level reliability of above 0.70, with all but one subdomain having a school-level reliability of above 0.75. This provides evidence that the CALL instrument is able to accomplish its most basic purpose of identifying the nature and existence of leadership practices within a school. Furthermore, we found that the CALL instrument is able to distinguish a substantial amount of between-school variation. In fact, 15 of the 20 subdomains on CALL demonstrate a between-school variation of above 0.15. The existence of high levels of between-school variation allows the CALL research team to investigate the relationships between school-level factors and leadership practices identified and measured by CALL.

The results from these analyses demonstrated that the CALL survey is a reliable instrument that can provide valuable formative assessment information to schools as well as meaningful data to researchers interested in school leadership

Table C.3 CALL Variance Decomposition

SUBDOMAIN	INDIVIDUAL LEVEL RELIABILITY	SCHOOL LEVEL RELIABILITY	LEVEL 1 VARIANCE COMPONENT	LEVEL 2 VARIANCE COMPONENT	PROPORTION OF VARIANCE BETWEEN INDIVIDUALS	PROPORTION OF VARIANCE BETWEEN SCHOOLS
1.1	0.74	0.865	0.194	0.055	0.778	0.222
1.2	0.79	0.867	0.257	0.075	0.773	0.227
1.3	0.67	0.898	0.333	0.14	0.704	0.296
1.4	0.74	0.713	0.325	0.032	0.911	0.089
2.1	0.7	0.858	0.227	0.063	0.782	0.218
2.2	0.56	0.884	0.303	0.109	0.736	0.264
2.3	0.7	0.88	0.382	0.135	0.739	0.261
2.4	0.83	0.913	0.188	0.097	0.661	0.339
3.1	0.76	0.82	0.189	0.04	0.825	0.175
3.2	0.7	0.832	0.519	0.122	0.81	0.19
3.3	0.86	0.778	0.35	0.051	0.873	0.127
3.4	0.8	0.874	0.162	0.055	0.746	0.254
4.1	0.66	0.762	0.427	0.06	0.876	0.124
4.2	0.72	0.789	0.442	0.075	0.856	0.144
4.3	0.81	0.84	0.256	0.064	0.801	0.199
4.4	0.61	0.837	0.329	0.074	0.816	0.184
4.5	0.7	0.798	0.122	0.022	0.847	0.153
5.1	0.77	0.83	0.205	0.044	0.825	0.175
5.2	0.9	0.864	0.132	0.042	0.757	0.243
5.3	0.75	0.76	0.123	0.017	0.878	0.122
Domain 1	0.798	0.864	0.098	0.028	0.779	0.221
Domain 2	0.86	0.906	0.098	0.045	0.683	0.317
Domain 3	0.842	0.845	0.085	0.02	0.805	0.195
Domain 4	0.848	0.83	0.108	0.023	0.824	0.176
Domain 5	0.726	0.837	0.108	0.025	0.816	0.184

practices. Specifically, the CALL subdomains and domains demonstrated high levels of statistical reliability as measured by both a traditional reliability assessment (Cronbach's alpha) and through an item response theory analysis using a Rasch model. Both of these analyses support the conceptualized constructs within the CALL instrument and that the items making up these constructs hang together as groups of leadership practices working toward common ends. Finally, through our HLM analysis, we demonstrated that CALL is reliable at the school level, which supports the notion that CALL accurately captures leadership practices within a school. In addition, our HLM analysis exhibited the power of CALL as a research tool because of its ability to differentiate among schools.

CALL Data and Mapping Leadership Book

The use of CALL has continued to grow. Data for the analyses in this book are drawn from surveys administered between 2013 and 2016, with 18,677 survey respondents from 611 schools in 14 states. Schools and districts that have taken the survey are a convenience sample in that the schools, districts, policymakers, leadership preparation programs, and school improvement networks opt in to administer the survey for many different purposes. We do not suggest that this is a representative sample of schools, but the schools draw from urban, suburban, and rural contexts and include schools at all levels of achievement and function. Urban districts, school improvement networks, and policymakers have administered CALL in very low-achieving schools; schools, districts, and school improvement networks have administered CALL in very high-achieving schools; and every other type of school in between. CALL schools operate in highly diverse and sometimes more homogeneous contexts. They include public schools, private schools, charter schools, and virtual schools. One thing that these schools have in common is a commitment to understand and improve leadership capacity. We believe these schools provide an important window on leadership practice that helps inform leaders, policymakers, and preparation programs about the current state of leadership practice and opportunities to strengthen leadership for learning in schools.

For more information about the CALL survey and professional development tools, see http://leadershipforlearning.org.

NOTES

1. Kelley, C., & Shaw, J. (2009).
2. Spillane, J. P., Halverson, R., & Diamond, J. B. (2004).

APPENDIX **D**

CALL Domains

Domain 1: Focus on Learning

1.1   Maintaining a schoolwide focus on learning

1.2   Recognition of formal leaders as instructional leaders

1.3   Collaborative design of integrated learning plan

1.4   Providing appropriate services for students who traditionally struggle

Domain 2: Monitoring Teaching and Learning

2.1   Formative evaluation of student learning

2.2   Summative evaluation of student learning

2.3   Formative evaluation of teaching

2.4   Summative evaluation of teaching

Domain 3: Building Professional Community

3.1   Collaborative schoolwide focus on problems of teaching and learning

3.2   Professional learning

3.3   Socially distributed leadership

3.4   Coaching and mentoring

Domain 4: Acquiring and Allocating Resources

4.1   Personnel practices

4.2   Structuring and maintaining time

4.3 School resources focus on student learning

4.4 Integrating external expertise into the school instructional program

4.5 Coordinating and supervising relations with families and external communities

Domain 5: Establishing a Safe and Effective Learning Environment

5.1 Clear, consistent, and enforced expectations for student behavior

5.2 Clean and safe learning environment

5.3 Support services for students who traditionally struggle

REFERENCES

Allensworth, E., & Easton, J. Q. (2007). *What matters for staying on-track and graduating in Chicago public high schools: A close look at course grades, failures and attendance in the freshman year.* Chicago, IL: Consortium on Chicago School Research.

Argyris, C., & Schön, D. A. (1974). *Theory in practice: Increasing professional effectiveness.* San Francisco, CA: Jossey-Bass.

Artiles, A. J., Bal, A., & King Thorius, K. A. (2010). Back to the future: A critique of response to intervention's social justice views. *Theory into Practice, 49*, 250–257.

Ashley, J., & Burke, K. (2010). *Implementing restorative justice: A field guide for schools.* Springfield: Illinois Criminal Justice Information Authority. https://www.sccgov.org/sites/pdo/ppw/SESAP/Documents/SCHOOL%20RJP%20GUIDEBOOOK.pdf

Baker, E. T. (1995). The effects of inclusion on learning. *Educational Leadership, 52*(4), 33–35.

Bal, A., King-Thorius, K. A., & Kozleski, E. (2012). *Culturally responsive positive behavioral support matters.* Tempe, AZ: Equity Alliance. Retrieved from http://www.equityallianceatasu.org/sites/default/files/CRPBIS_Matters.pdf

Balu, R., Zhu, P., Doolittle, F., Schiller, E., Jenkins, J., & Gersten, R. (2015). *Evaluation of response to intervention practices for elementary school reading* (NCEE 2016–4000). Washington, DC: National Center for Education Evaluation and Regional Assistance.

Barron, B. (2006). Interest and self-sustained learning as catalysts of development: A learning ecology perspective. *Human Development, 49*, 193–224.

Black, P., & Wiliam, D. (1998). Assessment and classroom learning. *Assessment in Education: Principles, policy and practice, 5*(1), 7–74.

Bolman, L. G., & Deal, T. E. (2008). *Reframing organizations: Artistry, choice, and leadership* (4th ed.). San Francisco, CA: Jossey-Bass.

Bowers, A. J. (2011). What's in a grade? The multidimensional nature of what teacher-assigned grades assess in high school. *Educational Research and Evaluation, 17*(3), 141–159.

Bowers, A. J., Blitz, M., Modest, M., Salisbury, J., & Halverson, R. (2017). How leaders agree with teachers in schools on measures of leadership practice: A two-level latent class analysis of the comprehensive assessment of leadership for learning. *Teachers College Record, 119*(1), 1–38.

Bradshaw, C. P., Mitchell, M. M., & Leaf, P. J. (2010). Examining the effects of school-wide positive behavioral interventions and supports on student outcomes: Results from a randomized controlled effectiveness trial in elementary schools. *Journal of Positive Behavior Interventions, 12*, 133–148.

Bryk, A., Camburn, E., & Louis, K. S. (1997). *Professional community in Chicago elementary schools: Facilitating factors and organizational consequences.* ERIC Document Reproduction Service No. ED 412, 624.

Bryk, A. S., Gomez, L., Grunow, A., & LeMahieu, P. (2015). *Learning to improve: How America's schools can get better at getting better.* Cambridge, MA: Harvard Education Publishing.

Bryk, A., & Schneider, B. (2002). *Trust in schools: A core resource for improvement.* New York, NY: Russell Sage Foundation.

Bryk, A. S., Sebring, P. B., Allensworth, E., Luppescu, S., & Easton, J. Q. (2010). *Organizing schools for improvement: Lessons from Chicago.* Chicago, IL: University of Chicago.

Burch, P. (2009). *Hidden markets: The new education privatization.* London: Routledge, Taylor & Francis.

Burris, C. C., & Welner, K. G. (2005). Closing the achievement gap by detracking. *Phi Delta Kappan, 86*(8), 594–598.

Butts, J. A., & Travis, J. (2002). *The rise and fall of American youth violence: 1980 to 2000.* Washington, DC: Urban Institute, Justice Policy Center.

Canole, M., & Young, M. (2013). *Standards for educational leaders: An analysis.* Washington, DC: Council of Chief State School Officers. Retrieved from http://www.ccsso.org/Documents/Analysis%20of%20Leadership%20Standards-Final-070913-RGB.pdf

Cantrell, S., & Kane, T. J. (2013). *Ensuring fair and reliable measures of effective teaching: Culminating findings from the MET Project's three-year study* (MET Project Policy and Practice Brief). Seattle, WA: Bill & Melinda Gates Foundation.

Carey, S. (1985). *Conceptual change in childhood.* Cambridge, MA: MIT Press.

Cavanagh, S. (2011, January 5). Personnel costs prove tough to contain, *Education Week Online.*

Chetty, R., Friedman, J. N., & Rockoff, J. E. (2012, January). *The long-term impacts of teachers: Teacher value-added and student outcomes in adulthood* (NBER Working Paper 17699). Cambridge, MA: NBER.

Chi, M.T.H., & Slotta, J. D. (1993). The ontological coherence of intuitive physics. *Cognition and Instruction, 10*(2 & 3), 249–260.

Christman, J., Neild, R., Bulkley, K., Blanc, S., Liu, R., Mitchell, C., & Travers, E. (2009). *Making the most of interim assessment data: Lessons from Philadelphia.* Philadelphia, PA: Research for Action.

City, E. A., Elmore, R. F., Fiarman, S. E. & Teitel, L. (2009). *Instructional rounds in education: A network approach to improving teaching and learning.* Cambridge, MA: Harvard Education Press.

Clinard, L. M., & Ariav, T. (1998). What mentoring does for mentors: A cross-cultural perspective. *European Journal of Teacher Education, 21*(1), 91–108.

Collins, J. (2001). *Good to great: Why some companies make the leap . . . and others don't.* New York: Harperbusiness.

Consortium for Chicago School Research. (2012). *The essential supports.* Retrieved from http://consortium.uchicago.edu/downloads/9954essentialsupports_onepager_final-2.pdf

Cornbleth, C. (2008). *Diversity and the new teacher: Learning from experience in urban schools.* New York, NY: Teachers College Press.

Crocco, M. S., & Costigan, A. T. (2007). The narrowing of curriculum and pedagogy in the age of accountability: Urban educators speak out. *Urban Education, 42*(6), 512–535.

Cross, C. T., & Donovan, M. S. (Eds.). (2002). *Minority students in special and gifted education.* Washington, DC: National Academies Press.

Danielson, C. (2011). *Enhancing professional practice: A framework for teaching.* Alexandria, VA: Association for Supervision and Curriculum Development.

Darling-Hammond, L., Amrein-Beardsley, A., Haertel, E. H., & Rothstein, J. (2011). *Getting teacher evaluation right: A background paper for policy makers.* Washington, DC: American Educational Research Association and National Academy of Education.

Darling-Hammond, L., Wei, R. C., Andree, A., Richardson, N., & Orphanos, S. (2009). *Professional learning in the learning profession: A status report on teacher development in the United States and abroad.* Dallas, TX: National Staff Development Council, and Stanford, CA: School Redesign Network.

Darling-Hammond, L., Wise, A. E., & Pease, S. R. (1983). Teacher evaluation in the organizational context: A review of the literature. *Review of Educational Research, 53(3),* 285–328.

Deal, T. E., & Peterson, K. D. (1994). *The leadership paradox: Balancing logic and artistry in schools.* San Francisco, CA: Jossey-Bass.

DeAngelis, K. J., & Presley, J. B. (2011). Teacher qualifications and school climate: Examining their interrelationship for school improvement. *Leadership and Policy in Schools, 10*(1), 84–120.

DiSessa, A. A. (2001). *Changing minds: Computers, learning, and literacy.* Cambridge, MA: MIT Press.

Downey, C. J., Steffy, B. E., English, F. W., Frase, L. E., & Poston, W. K. (2004). *The three-minute classroom walkthrough: Changing school supervisory practice one teacher at a time.* Thousand Oaks, CA: Corwin Press.

Dunlosky, J., Rawson, K. A., Marsh, E. J., Nathan, M. J., & Willingham, D. T. (2011). Improving students' learning with effective learning techniques: Promising directions from cognitive and educational psychology. *Psychological Science in the Public Interest, 14*(1), 4–58.

Elmore, R. (2000). *Building a new structure for school leadership.* Washington, DC: Albert Shanker Institute.

Elmore, R. F., & Fuhrman, S. H. (2001). Holding schools accountable: Is it working? *Phi Delta Kappan, 83*(1), 67–70, 72.

Fabelo, T., Thompson, M. D., Plotkin, M., Carmichael, D., Marchbanks III, M. P., & Booth, E. A. (2011). *Breaking schools' rules: A statewide study of how school discipline relates to students' success and juvenile justice involvement.* New York, NY: Council of State Governments Justice Center.

Farris-Berg, K., Dirkswager, E. J., & Junge, A. (2012). *Trusting teachers with school success: What happens when teachers call the shots.* Lanham, MD: R&L Education.

Fosnot, C. (1996). *Constructivism: Theory, perspectives, and practice.* New York, NY: Teachers College Press.

Fullan, M., & Knight, J. (2011). Coaches as system leaders. *Educational Leadership, 69*(2), 50–53.

Gallucci, C., Van Lare, M. D., Yoon, I. H., & Boatright, B. (2010). Instructional coaching building theory about the role and organizational support for professional learning. *American Educational Research Journal, 47*(4), 919–963.

Gamoran, A. (2009). *Tracking and inequality: New directions for research and practice* (WCER Working Paper 2009–6). Madison: University of Wisconsin–Madison, Wisconsin Center for Education Research. Retrieved from http://www.wcer.wisc.edu/publications/workingPapers/papers.php

Gardner, H. (1995). *Leading minds: An anatomy of leadership.* New York: Basic Books.

Gee, J. P. (2007). *What video games have to teach us about learning and literacy* (2nd ed.). London: St. Martin's.

Gersten, R., Compton, D., Connor, C. M., Dimino, J., Santoro, L., Linan-Thompson, S., & Tilly, W. D. (2008). *Assisting students struggling with reading: Response to intervention and multi-tier intervention for reading in the primary grades. A practice guide* (NCEE 2009–4045). Washington, DC: National Center for Education Evaluation and Regional Assistance, Institute of Education Sciences, U.S. Department of Education. Retrieved from http://ies.ed.gov/ncee/wwc/publications/practiceguides

Ginsberg, M. B., & Murphy, D. (2002). How walkthroughs open doors. *Educational Leadership, 59*(8), 34–36.

Glazerman, S., Goldhaber, D., Loeb, S., Raudenbush, S., Staiger, D. O., Whitehurst, G. J., & Croft, M. (2011). *Passing muster: Evaluating teacher evaluation systems.* Washington, DC: Brookings Institution.

Goff, P. T., Goldring, E., & Bickman, L. (2014). Predicting the gap: Perceptual congruence between American principals and their teachers' ratings of leadership effectiveness. *Education Assessment Evaluation and Accountability 26*(4), 333–359.

Gonzalez, T. (2015). Socializing schools: Addressing racial disparities in discipline through restorative justice. In D. J. Losen (Ed.), *Closing the school discipline gap: Equitable remedies for excessive exclusion.* New York, NY: Teachers College Press.

Gordon, S., & Maxey, S. (2000). *How to help beginning teachers succeed* (2nd ed.). Alexandria, VA: Association for Supervision and Curriculum Development.

Gresham, F. M. (2007). Evolution of the response-to-intervention concept: Empirical foundations and recent developments. In S. R. Jimerson, M. K. Burns, & A. M. VanDerHeyden (Eds.), *Handbook of response to intervention: The science and practice of assessment and intervention* (pp. 10–24). London: Springer.

Grissom, J. A., Loeb, S., & Master, B. (2013). Effective instructional time use for school leaders: Longitudinal evidence from observations of principals. *Educational Researcher, 42*(8), 433–444.

Grossman, P., Schoenfeld, A., & Lee, C. (2007). Teaching subject matter. In L. Darling-Hammond & J. Bransford (Eds.), *Preparing teachers for a changing world: What teachers should know and be able to do* (pp. 201–231). New York, NY: Wiley.

Hallinger, Philip. (1992). The evolving role of American principals: From managerial to instructional to transformational leaders. *Journal of Educational Administration, 30*(3), 35. Retrieved from ProQuest.

Hallinger, P., & Heck, R. H. (1998). Exploring the principal's contribution to school effectiveness: 1980–1995. *School Effectiveness and School Improvement, 9*(2), 157–191.

Halverson, R., Grigg, J., Prichett, R., & Thomas, C. (2007). The new instructional leadership: Creating data-driven instructional systems in school. *Journal of School Leadership, 17*(2), 159–193.

Halverson, R., Kallio, J., Hackett, S., & Halverson, E. (2016). *Participatory culture as a model for how new media technologies can change public Schools* (WCER Working Paper 2016–7). Retrieved from http://www.wcer.wisc.edu/publications/working-papers/

Halverson, R., Kelley, C., & Kimball, S. (2004). Implementing teacher evaluation systems: How principals make sense of complex artifacts to shape local instructional practice. In W. K. Hoy & C. G. Miskel (Eds.), *Educational administration, policy and reform: Research and measurement research and theory in educational administration* (Vol. 3). Greenwich, CT: Information Age Press.

Halverson, R., Prichett, R. & Watson, J. G. (2007). *Formative feedback systems and the new instructional leadership* (WCER Working Paper). Madison: Wisconsin Center for Educational Research. Retrieved from http://www.wcer.wisc.edu/Publications/workingPapers/Working_Paper_No_2007_03.swf

Halverson, R., & Thomas, C. (2007). The roles and practices of student services staff as data-driven instructional leaders. In M. Mangin & S. Stoelinga (Eds.), *Instructional teachers' leadership roles: Using research to inform and reform* (pp. 163–200). New York, NY: Teachers College Press.

Hanushek, E. A., & Rivkin, S. G. (2010). Generalizations about using value-added measures of teacher quality. *American Economic Review, 100*(2), 267–271.

Herman, J. L., Osmundson, E., & Dietel, R. (2010). *Benchmark assessments for improved learning* (AACC Policy Brief). Los Angeles: University of California.

Hoffmann, J. P., Erickson, L. D., & Spence, K. R. (2013). Modeling the association between academic achievement and delinquency: An application of interactional theory. *Criminology, 51*, 629–660.

Horng, E., & Loeb, S. (2010). New thinking about instructional leadership. *Phi Delta Kappan, 92*(3), 66–69.

Huling, L., & Resta, V. (2001). Teacher mentoring as professional development. *ERIC Digest. ERIC Clearinghouse on Teaching and Teacher Education.* Retrieved from http://www.ericdigests.org/2002-3/mentoring.htm

Hurd, J., & Lewis, C. (2011). *Lesson study step by step: How teacher learning communities improve instruction.* Portsmouth, NH: Heinemann Press.

Hutchins, E. (1995). *Cognition in the wild.* Cambridge, MA: MIT Press.

Ingersoll, R. (2007). Short on power, long on responsibility. *Educational Leadership 65*(1), 20–25.

Ingersoll, R. (2012). Beginning teacher induction: What the data tell us. *Phi Delta Kappan, 93*(8), 47–51.

Ingersoll, R., & Kralik, J. M. (2004). *The impact of mentoring on teacher retention: What the research says.* Denver, CO: Education Commission of the States.

Ingersoll, R., & May, H. (2011). *Recruitment, retention, and the minority teacher shortage.* Philadelphia: University of Pennsylvania, Consortium for Policy Research in Education.

Ingersoll, R., & Perda, D. (2010). Is the supply of mathematics and science teachers sufficient? *American Educational Research Journal, 47*(3), 563–595.

Irby, J. D. (2013). Net-deepening of school discipline. *Urban Review, 45*, 197–219.

Irby, J. D. (2014). Trouble at school: Understanding school discipline systems as nets of social control. *Equity and Excellence in Education, 47*(4), 513–530.

Ito, M., Gutiérrez, K., Livingstone, S., Penuel, B., Rhodes, J., Salen, K., Schor, J., . . . Watkins, S. C. (2013). *Connected learning: An agenda for research and design.* Irvine, CA: Digital Media and Learning Research Hub.

Kamenetz, A. (2015). *The test: Why our schools are obsessed with standardized testing—but you don't have to be.* New York, NY: Public Affairs.

Kane, T. J., McCaffrey, D. F., Miller, T., & Staiger, D. O. (2013). *Have we identified effective teachers? Validating measures of effective teaching using random assignment (MET Project Research Paper).* Seattle, WA: Bill & Melinda Gates Foundation.

Kane, T. J., Taylor, E. S., Tyler, J. H., & Wooten, A. L. (2011). Identifying effective classroom practices using student achievement data. *Journal of Human Resources, 46*(3), 587–613.

Kang-Brown, J., Trone, J., Fratello, J., & Daftary-Kapur, T. (2013, December). *A generation later: What we've learned about zero tolerance in schools* (Vera Foundation Policy Issue Brief). New York, NY: Vera Foundation.

Kelley, C., & Dikkers, S. (2016). Framing feedback for school improvement around distributed leadership. *Educational Administration Quarterly, 52,* 392–422.

Kelley, C., Heneman, H. G. III, & Milanowski, A. (2002). Teacher motivation and school-based performance awards. *Educational Administration Quarterly, 38*(3), 372–401.

Kelley, C., & Shaw, J. (2009). *Learning first! A school leader's guide to closing achievement gaps.* Thousand Oaks, CA: Corwin.

Lee, V. E., & Smith, J. B. (1996). Collective responsibility for learning and its effects on gains in achievement for early secondary school students. *American Journal of Education, 104*(2), 103–147.

Leithwood, K. (2001). School leadership in the context of accountability policies. *International Journal of Leadership in Education, 4*(3), 217–235.

Leithwood, K., & Riehl, C. (2005). *What do we already know about school leadership? A new agenda: Directions for research on educational leadership.* New York, NY: Teachers College Press.

Lewis, A. E., & Diamond, J. B. (2015). *Despite the best intentions: How racial inequality thrives in good schools.* Oxford: Oxford University Press.

Lezotte, L. W., & Jacoby, B. C. (1990). *The school improvement process based on effective schools research: A guide.* Okemos, MI: Effective Schools Products.

Lezotte, L. W., & Snyder, K. M. (2011). *What effective schools do: Re-envisioning the correlates.* Bloomington, IN: Solution Tree Press.

Little, J. W. (1982). Norms of collegiality and experimentation: Workplace conditions of school success. *American Educational Research Journal, 19*(3), 325–340.

Livermore, C. (2008). Unrelenting expectations: A more nuanced understanding of the broken windows theory of cultural management in urban education. *University of Pennsylvania Graduate School of Education Perspectives on Urban Education, 5*(2), 2.

Los Angeles Unified School District Board of Education. (2013, May 14). *School discipline policy and school climate bill of rights* (Board Resolution). Retrieved from http://209.80.43.43/ SchoolDisciplinePolicyandSchoolClimateBillofRights2013.pdf

Losen, D. J., Hodson, C. L., Keith, I. I., Michael, A., Morrison, K., & Belway, S. (2015). *Are we closing the school discipline gap?* Los Angeles: Civil Rights Project, UCLA. Retrieved from https://www.civilrightsproject. ucla.edu/resources/projects/center-for-civil-rights-remedies/ school-to-prison-folder/federal-reports/are-we-closing-the-school-discipline-gap

Louis, K. S., Kruse, S., & Bryk, A. S. (1995). Professionalism and community: What is it and why is it important in urban schools? In K. S. Louis & S. Kruse (Eds.), *Professionalism and community* (pp. 3–22). Thousand Oaks, CA: Sage.

Louis, K. S., Marks, H. M., & Kruse, S. (1996). Teachers' professional community in restructuring schools. *American Educational Research Journal, 33*(4), 757–798.

Loup, K. S., Garland, J. S., Ellett, C. D., & Rugutt, J. K. (1996). Ten years later: Findings from a replication of a study of teacher evaluation practices in our 100 largest school districts. *Journal of Personnel Evaluation in Education, 10*, 203–226.

Mangin, M. M. (2014). Capacity building and districts' decision to implement coaching initiatives. *Education Policy Analysis Archives, 22*(56), 1–25.

Mangin, M. M., & Dunsmore, K. (2015). How the framing of instructional coaching as a lever for systemic or individual reform influences the enactment of coaching. *Educational Administration Quarterly, 51*(2), 179–213.

Marzano, R. J. (2005). *School leadership that works.* Alexandria, VA: ASCD.

Maslow, A. (1954). *Motivation and personality.* New York, NY: Harper.

McCluskey, G., Lloyd, G., Kane, J., Riddell, S., Stead, J., & Weedon, E. (2008). Can restorative practices in schools make a difference? *Educational Review, 60*(4), 405–417.

Means, B., Padilla, C., & Gallagher, L. (2010). *Use of education data at the local level from accountability to instructional improvement.* Washington, DC: U.S. Department of Education, Office of Planning, Evaluation, and Policy Development.

Mehan, H., Mercer, J., & Rueda, R. (2002). Special education. In D. L. Levinson, P. W. Cookson, & A. R. Sadovnik (Eds.), *Education and sociology* (pp. 619–624). New York, NY: Routledge Falmer.

Meyer, H. D., & Rowan, B. (2006). *The new institutionalism in education.* Albany: State University of New York Press.

Miles, K. H., & Frank, S. (2008). *The strategic school: Making the most of people, time, and money.* Thousand Oaks, CA: Corwin.

Milner, H. R. (2013). *Policy reforms and de-professionalization of teaching.* Boulder, CO: National Education Policy Center. Retrieved from http://nepc.colorado.edu/publication/policy-reforms-deprofessionalization

Modeste, M. & Kelley, C. (2015, November). *Examining distributed leadership practices by school grade-configuration using the Comprehensive Assessment of Leadership for Learning.* Paper presented at the University Council for Educational Administration Conference, San Diego, CA.

Nardi, B. A., & O'Day, V. L. (1999) *Information ecologies: Using technology with heart.* Cambridge, MA: MIT Press.

National Center for Education Statistics. (2015). *Children and youth with disabilities.* Washington, DC: Author. Retrieved from http://nces.ed.gov/programs/coe/indicator_cgg.asp

National Council on Teacher Quality. (2013). *2012 state teacher policy yearbook: Improving teacher preparation.* Washington, DC: Author.

Nelson, B. S., & Sassi, A. (2005). *The effective principal: Instructional leadership for high-quality learning.* New York, NY: Teachers College Press.

Newmann, F. M. (1996). *Authentic achievement: Restructuring schools for intellectual quality.* San Francisco: Jossey-Bass.

Newmann, F. M., & Wehlage, G. G. (1995). *Successful school restructuring: A report to the public and educators.* Madison: Center on Organization and Restructuring of Schools, University of Wisconsin–Madison.

Nichols, S. L., & Berliner, D. C. (2005). *The inevitable corruption of indicators and educators through high-stakes testing.* Tempe: Education Policy Studies Laboratory Division of Educational Leadership and Policy Studies, Arizona State University.

Odden, A. (2011). *Strategic management of human capital in education: Improving instructional practice and student learning in schools.* New York, NY: Routledge.

Odden, A., & Kelley, C. (2002). *Paying teachers for what they know and do: New and smarter compensation strategies to improve performance.* Thousand Oaks, CA: Corwin.

Peterson, K. D. (1989). *Secondary principals and instructional leadership: Complexities in a diverse role.* Madison: National Center on Effective Secondary Schools, University of Wisconsin–Madison.

Peterson, K. D. (1995). *Teacher evaluation: A comprehensive guide to new directions and practices.* Thousand Oaks, CA: Corwin.

Pianta, R. C., Mashburn, A. J., Downer, J. T., Hamre, B. K., & Justice, L. (2008). Effects of web-mediated professional development resources on teacher-child interactions in pre-kindergarten classrooms. *Early Childhood Research Quarterly, 23*(4), 431–451.

Porter, A., Murphy, J., Goldring, E., Elliot, S., Polikoff, M. S., & May, H. (2008). *Vanderbilt Assessment of Leadership in Education: Technical manual.* Nashville, TN: Vanderbilt University.

Prichett, R. (2007). *How school leaders make sense of and use formative feedback systems.* Unpublished doctoral dissertation, University of Wisconsin–Madison School of Education.

Protheroe, N. (2009). Using classroom walkthroughs to improve instruction. *Principal, 88*(4), 30–34.

Raiford, S. A. (2004). *The relationship between span of control and school performance in selected high and low achieving public elementary schools in Florida* (Doctoral dissertation). Retrieved from ProQuest (3137379).

Rebora, A. (2010, April 12). Responding to RTI: Interview with Richard Allington. *Education Week.*

Reitzug, U. C. (1994). A study of empowering principal behavior. *American Educational Research Journal, 31*(2), 283–307.

Reitzug, U. C., & Reeves, J. E. (1992). "Miss Lincoln doesn't teach here": A descriptive narrative and conceptual analysis of a principal's symbolic leadership behavior. *Educational Administration Quarterly, 28*(2), 185–219.

Resnick, L. B., & Glennan, T. K. (2002). Leadership for learning: A theory of action for urban school districts. In A. T. Hightower, M. S. Knapp, J. A. Marsh, & M. W. McLaughlin (Eds.), *School districts and instructional renewal* (pp. 160–172). New York, NY: Teachers College Press.

Robers, S., Kemp, J., & Truman, J. (2013). *Indicators of school crime and safety: 2012* (NCES 2013–036/NCJ 241446). Washington, DC: National Center for Education Statistics.

Ruijs, N. M., & Peetsma, T. T. (2009). Effects of inclusion on students with and without special educational needs reviewed. *Educational Research Review, 4*(2), 67–79.

Salisbury, J., Camburn, E., Kelley, C., Halverson, R., Goff, P., Kimball, S., . . . Durga, S. (2013). *The Comprehensive Assessment of Leadership for Learning: Technical report.* Madison: Wisconsin Center for Education Research, University of Wisconsin-Madison.

Sebastian, J., & Allensworth, E. (2012). The influence of principal leadership on classroom instruction and student learning: A study of mediated pathways to learning. *Educational Administration Quarterly, 48*(4), 626–663.

Shah, N. (2011, August 19). Survey of school, district workers shows wider use of RtI. *Education Week, 1.* Retrieved from http://blogs.edweek.org/edweek/speced/2011/08/yet_another_study_shows_the.html

Shepard, L. (2010). What the marketplace has brought us: Item-by-item teaching with little instructional insight. *Peabody Journal of Education, 85*(2), 246–257.

Sherin, M. G., & van Es, E. A. (2009). Effects of video club participation on teachers' professional vision. *Journal of Teacher Education, 60,* 20–37.

Skiba, R. J., Peterson, R. L., & Williams, T. (1997). Office referrals and suspension: Disciplinary intervention in middle schools. *Education and Treatment of Children, 20,* 295–315.

Slavin, R. E. (2002). Evidence-based education policies: Transforming educational practice and research. *Educational Researcher, 31*(7), 15–21.

Smith, J. P., diSessa, A. A., & Roschelle, J. (1993). Misconceptions reconceived: A constructivist analysis of knowledge in transition. *Journal of Learning and Sciences, 3*(2), 115–163.

Spillane, J. P. (2006). *Distributed leadership.* San Francisco, CA: Jossey-Bass.

Spillane, J. P., Halverson, R., & Diamond, J. B. (2001). Investigating school leadership practice: A distributed perspective. *Educational Researcher, 30*(3), 23–28.

Spillane, J. P., Halverson, R., & Diamond, J. B. (2004). Towards a theory of leadership practice: A distributed perspective. *Journal of Curriculum Studies, 36*(1), 3–34.

Spillane, J. P., Parise, L. M., & Sherer, J. Z. (2011). Organizational routines as coupling mechanisms: Policy, school administration, and the technical core. *American Educational Research Journal, 48*(3), 586–619.

Sugai, G., & Horner, R. (2006). A promising approach for expanding and sustaining the implementation of school-wide positive behavior support. *School Psychology Review, 35,* 245–259.

Supovitz, J. A., & Poglinco, S. M. (2001). *Instructional leadership in a standards-based reform.* Philadelphia, PA: Consortium for Policy Research in Education.

Thomas, C. (2007). *Problem-solving teams and data-driven school leadership: A path toward the next generation of special education services.* Doctoral dissertation, University of Wisconsin–Madison School of Education.

Tomlinson, C. A. (1999). *The differentiated classroom: Responding to the needs of all learners.* Alexandria, VA: Association for Supervision and Curriculum Development.

Tough, P. (2012). *How children succeed: Grit, curiosity and the hidden power of character.* New York, NY: Houghton Mifflin Harcourt.

Turnbull, B. J., Haslam, M. B., Arcaira, E. R., Riley, D. L., Sinclair, B., & Coleman, S. (2009). *Evaluation of the School Administration Manager Project.* Washington, DC: Policy Studies Associates.

U.S. Department of Justice. (2014). *Juvenile arrests 2012* (Juvenile Offenders and Victims: National Report Series). Retrieved from https://www.ojjdp.gov/pubs/248513.pdf

van Es, E. A., & Sherin, M. G. (2010). The influence of video clubs on teachers' thinking and practice. *Journal of Math Teacher Education, 13*, 155–176.

Vroom, V. H., & Deci, E. L. (1983). *Management and motivation.* New York, NY: Penguin.

Wahba, M. A., & Bridwell, L. G. (1976). Maslow reconsidered: A review of research on the need hierarchy theory. *Organizational Behavior and Human Performance, 15*(2), 212–240.

Wallace, K. (2015, April 24). Parents all over U.S. "opting out" of standardized student testing. *CNN.* Retrieved from http://www.cnn.com/2015/04/17/living/parents-movement-opt-out-of-testing-feat/

Wallace Foundation. (2011). *The school principal as leader: Guiding schools to better teaching and learning.* Retrieved from http://www.wallacefoundation.org/knowledge-center/school-leadership/effective-principal-leadership/Documents/The-School-Principal-as-Leader-Guiding-Schools-to-Better-Teaching-and-Learning.pdf

Watanabe, T. (2013, May 12). LAUSD board could ban suspensions for "willful defiance." *Los Angeles Times.* Retrieved from http://articles.latimes.com/2013/may/12/local/la-me-adv-lausd-discipline-20130513

Weick, K. (1976). Educational organizations as loosely coupled systems. *Administrative Science Quarterly, 21*(1), 1–19.

Weick, K. (1999). *Sensemaking in organizations.* Thousand Oaks, CA: Sage.

Weingarten, R. (2015). Moving past punishment to support. *American Educator, 39*(4), 1–2. Retrieved from www.aft.org/ae

Wenger, E. (1998). *Communities of practice: Learning, meaning, and identity.* Cambridge: Cambridge University Press.

Yoon, K. S., Duncan, T., Lee, S. W.-Y., Scarloss, B., & Shapley, K. (2007). *Reviewing the evidence on how teacher professional development affects student achievement* (Issues & Answers Report, REL 2007–No. 033). Washington, DC: U.S. Department of Education, Institute of Education Sciences, National Center for Education Evaluation and Regional Assistance, Regional Educational Laboratory Southwest. Retrieved from http://ies.ed.gov/ncee/edlabs

Youngs, P., & King, M. B. (2002). Principal leadership for professional development to build school capacity. *Educational Administration Quarterly, 38*(5), 643–670.

Zehr, H. (1997). Restorative justice: The concept. *Corrections Today, 59*(7), 68–70.

INDEX

Page references followed by Fig indicate an illustrated figure and Tab indicate table

Printed and bound by CPI Group (UK) Ltd, Croydon, CR0 4YY

25/03/2025

14647353-0001